Neural Representations o
Uncertainty in Huma

Emanuele De Luca

Table of Contents

List of Figures

10

11

cortical and subcortical. Each group is also paired with a response profile type (either linear or quadratic) as found in our analysis of outcome anticipation (Fig. 5.3 and 5.4). Overall the model shows differences in connectivity between the social and non-social domain. Not only functional connectivity differs in cortical regions but most importantly between these and the subcortical regions, proving further evidence to interpret the different response profile found for social and non-social uncertainty. Regions abbreviations: aIns (anterior insula); dACC (dorsal anterior cingulate cortex); OFC (orbitofrontal cortex); mPFC (medial prefrontal cortex); VS (ventral striatum)..100

13

activation in bilateral anterior insula (aIns) and dorsal anterior cingulate cortex (dACC) during outcome anticipation for TG-Trust and NoTrust trials is lower at onset for low RePE and higher for high RePE regardless of the expected fairness of trustee. At outcome delivery this tendency is inverted. Here neural activation for both TG Trust and NoTrust conditions is higher when trustee's answer is unfair (red) and lower when it is fair (green), regardless of the actual outcome and monetary gain.135

(light blue). Plots show that similarly to what found in dACC, neural activation in a cluster of the cuneus (x=-12; y=-72; z=22; 250 voxels; max stat=5.02) to card game trials (CG) correlates positively with risk prediction error after first card. This first prediction error update is represented as a U-shaped function of 10 reward probability conditions (top plot; x-axis represents probability of winning; dotted line best quadratic fit; see also Methods). Activation in the same cluster to both trust game subgroups of trials (TG-Trust and TG-NoTrust) correlates positively with a linear function of reward probability conditions as of display of trustee's face (top plots; x-axis, from left to right, represents ascending reward probability conditions; dotted lines best linear fit). Bottom plots represent the same type of effect by averaging CG and TG conditions in 3 bins representing 3 ascending levels of reward probability (see also Methods)...158

List of Tables

I Decision Making under Social and Non-Social Uncertainty

Part I Overview

Human beings evolved an ability to navigate a world filled with different forms of uncertainty. Every day people make plans and perform actions that involve other people, be it deciding for them, together with them or just taking into account their judgements. At the same time we have an ability for abstraction and make decisions that might not have a social content (e.g. playing a hand of poker with a computer or building an investment portfolio that would return the highest financial profit).

Until recently the brain mechanisms underlying social and non-social types of choices have been examined from different theoretical angles. In the non-social domain of decision-making (for example, when playing probabilistic games), scientists have often focused on the neural code underlying value computations associated with the rewarding properties of the choice. By contrast, researchers studying social decisions (for example, playing games with a human opponent) have often focused on neural processes that may have evolved to guide social behaviour. On the one hand, non-social oriented research led to the discovery of brain regions involved in value computation and to the idea of a common currency system evaluating the motivational relevance of any kind of stimuli (Chapter 1). On the other hand, social oriented research exposed a number of brain structures specifically involved in representing intentions, emotions or actions of other people, leading to the idea of a social specific type of cognition (Chapter 2). More recently studies comparing social and non-social types of decision-making have challenged such dichotomy and suggested social decisions may also depend on value-related neural processes in use during non-social decisions (Chapter 3).

A further important development is that of theories trying to unite in a single comprehensive framework not only social and non-social factors, but more in general the common neural mechanism underlying all decision making processes in the brain. For instance, recent predictive coding accounts propose a common model to study perceptual, cognitive and motivational aspects of brain function where at the centre are prediction and prediction error units. Such endeavour has been greatly inspired by work in visual neuroscience focussing on the cortical area known as visual area 1 or V1 (Chapter 4).

1 Neural Basis of Reward Processing under Non-Social Decision Making

Today neuroscientists know much about how humans and other animals learn the value of their actions. Key to this scientific revolution was the discovery that dopamine neurons encode a reward prediction error signal. Researchers had long hypothesised that the neurotransmitter dopamine played a critical role in processing rewards (Wise & Rompre 1989). Still the most common view was that dopaminergic neurons were the pleasure centre of the brain. The problem with this hypothesis was that although it was true that humans or animals would actively seek to activate these neurons in experimental settings, primary rewards such as food or water did not reliably activate these neurons. For instance, it was demonstrated that when rats were placed in a novel environment, dopamine neurons would be active when food and water were first discovered, but that activity dramatically decreased as the animals became accustomed to finding and consuming those rewards (Fibiger & Phillips 2011). As the idea that dopamine equalled reward per se was being abandoned by the scientific community, other alternative hypotheses were proposed. One of these argued that dopamine neurons encoded salience (Horvitz 2000; Redgrave et al. 1999), rather than coding reward per se. In other words activity recorded encoded how strongly events in the world deviated from expectations, whether those expectations were positive or negative. This hypothesis could explain why the dopamine neurons responded so strongly when a rat entered a novel environment and encountered food and water, but were later silent. Initially the discovery of food was a surprise, but after days of finding food in the same place, the salience of that observation was very low and this was reflected in threshold spike activity. However, though the notion of salience encoding would later become a complementary hypothesis on its own, it had some crucial problems when used to explain reward processing. Among all, the simple fact that a salience hypothesis would separate the activity of dopamine neurons from the same notion of reward. In this climate the work of primate neurophysiologist Wolfram Schultz proved to be crucial.

1.1 Reward processing and the notion of reward and risk prediction errors

Our current understanding of the fast (phasic) dopamine signals are based on almost thirty years of experimental work, particularly on the remarkable experiments conducted in Schultz's laboratory. They recorded the activity of single dopamine neurons in the brain of the monkey while the primate participated in Pavlovian conditioning tasks (Mirenowicz & Schultz 1994; Schultz et al. 1997). In these early experiments the animal would sit in front of a water or juice releasing spout and at unpredictable intervals, a sound was produced and a drop of water would be provided to the thirsty monkey. Initially dopamine neurons would fire at 3 to 5 Hz when the tone was played, and responded with a much higher-frequency burst of action potentials when the water was delivered. After several repetitions the neurons would respond with a much higher frequency to the unpredictable sound preceding the rewarding water drops. Concurrently the neurons started to be unaffected by the water delivery as they maintained their baseline firing rate during the actual delivery of reward. Crucially, if the experimenter delivered a drop of water not preceded by the sound, then the dopamine neurons would again respond to the unpredictable reward with a burst of action potentials. Omission of the reward, when this was expected based on the preceding sound, resulted in a reduced response below baseline (Fig.1.1). This and several other variants of the same experiment (Schultz 2013) clearly indicated that it was not the reward itself that had lost the ability to activate the dopamine neurons, rather the monkey had learned to expect that reward and this resulted in a baseline activity of the dopamine neurons recorded.

In parallel, theories of learning had recently emerged from computer science. Temporal difference (TD) learning (Sutton & Barto 1998), a form of reinforcement learning, was an extension of the Rescorla-Wagner rule (Rescorla & Wagner 1972) whose goal is to predict future rewards by continuously comparing incoming rewards with predictions. The resulting error is then used to update predictions about future rewards. In a remarkable example of cross-disciplinary collaboration, a group of researchers recognised the similarity of the phasic response in dopamine neurons with the error term used in TD models and this led to the reward prediction error hypothesis (Schultz et al. 1997). Importantly, the firing rates of the dopamine neurons were predicted by this pre-existing theory of learning. It was then clear that phasic dopamine responses encoded a prediction error about the summed future rewards. Thus

TD models formally showed how prediction errors signalled by dopamine neurons are the result of the continuous comparison of predictions of reward with actual rewards.

In more recent years research drawing from economics and financial decision theory has led to further important advancements in the understanding of the theory of learning and the neural underpinnings of motivational behaviour under uncertainty. Before introducing these results, a brief reference to some keys concepts that shaped the current neuroeconomic approach to the theory of choice under uncertainty is presented. (Note that in the context of the present work we distinguish between choices under risk, when the probability distribution of potential outcomes are known to the decision maker, and decisions under ambiguity, when probabilities are unknown. We use the term uncertainty to refer in general to any form of risky decision-making).

Methods for choosing between actions with probabilistic outcomes have been extensively developed since Pascal's original formulation, when in mid 17th century he employed the emerging probability theory to postulate a formal description of decision-making. In essence Pascal suggested that choices are the sum of the value of all possible events weighted by the probability of their occurrence. So choices are based on expectations, hence the concept of expected value (EV). Given all possible outcomes, each having the probability $p(x)$ of occurring, the EV is given by the sum of all possible outcomes each weighted by their probability $p(x)$.

$$EV(x) = \sum_x p(x) \cdot x$$

It was not until Bernoulli's formulation (Bernoulli 1954) that the idea of utility was introduced. In fact, EV was rejected as a universally applicable decision criterion based on the St. Petersburg paradox, where people are found to be willing to pay only a small price when playing games with a highly skewed payoff distribution that has infinite expected value. This led to replace this measurable external world variable called value with a mathematically transformed version hidden inside the chooser. Importantly this new variable, utility, could account for the observed aversion of humans to risky decision-making. The theory of expected utility would not receive an axiomatic formulation until a couple of hundred years

26

later (Von Neumann & Morgenstern 1944). Crucially, in their formulation John von Neumann and Oskar Morgenstern included choices with uncertain outcomes. In other words they defined the type of objects people would be asked to choose so that uncertain events could be studied and related. To do so they formally described an object of choice called lottery defined by two numbers: a probability and a value. In analogy to the theory of expected value, expected utility (EU) sums the utilities u(x) of all possible outcomes of a choice, weighted by their probability of occurrence.

$$EU(x) = \sum_x p(x) \cdot u(x)$$

Since then a number of scientific studies have gone into applying approaches rooted in this theory of optimal choice to model human decisions under risk.

Importantly, in the economic framework often the goal is to find a mathematical function that satisfies all axioms and at the same time is a good fit of different forms of decision-making behaviour under risk. However, how probability and risk are exactly integrated and give rise to that function is not known. The economic approach therefore models expected reward and risk implicitly.

There is an alternative approach to model choice under uncertainty rooted in financial decision theory where these two parameters are modelled explicitly. This approach assumes that risky options are not represented as outcome-probability pairs (EU theory) but as outcome distributions that can be described by their moments, and in particular their mean (first moment) and their variance (the second moment). The two important ideas that will be later borrowed by neuroscientists are that preferences can be accurately described using only the expected return (expected reward or mean) and risk is measured as variance. These concepts have been introduced by Henry Markowitz in his work on portfolio selection (Markowitz 1952; Markowitz 1959). The theory modelled people's willingness to pay (WTP) for risky options as a trade-off between the option's first moment, its mean return V(x), and its second moment, its risk R(x), defined as the variance of outcomes - the assumption here is that people would try to minimise level of risk for a given level of return. (Note there is also a measure of risk attitude, with positive b coefficients denoting risk-aversion and negative coefficients denoting risk seeking).

27

$$WTP(x) = V(x) - bR(x)$$

In recent years the neuroeconomic community translated this risk-return framework into testable hypotheses showing that there is indeed evidence of explicit neural representations of expected reward and risk, when expected rewards are measured as the mean and risk is measured as the variance of outcomes (Preuschoff et al. 2006; Schultz et al. 2008). Interestingly, it has been proposed that any system engaged in effective reinforcement learning should not only encode reward prediction errors but also prediction risk and that this metric can be used to scale risk prediction errors (Preuschoff & Bossaerts 2007).

The following section gives an overview of the brain structures involved in reward and risk processing. Some of the more recent studies will be related to the research presented in later chapters.

1.2 Reward and risk processing structures

A large body of literature seems to indicate that dopamine neurons form a specialised low-bandwidth channel for broadcasting the same information to large territories in the basal ganglia and frontal cortex. The majority of dopamine neurons reside in the midbrain and form three cell groups, the retrorubral nucleus (RRN; cell group A8), the substantia nigra pars compacta (SNpc; A9), and the ventral tegmental area (VTA; A10). From these small nuclei, the dopamine neurons send their widespread, ascending projections to the dorsal and ventral striatum, dorsolateral and orbital prefrontal cortex and other cortical and subcortical structures (Fig.1.2).

The anatomy of the dopaminergic system is reflected in the findings of a large number of electrophysiological and neuroimaging experiments studying reward function. Brain regions that respond to rewards include ventral tegmental area (Romo & Schultz 1990), the caudate, putamen and ventral striatum (Apicella et al. 1991), subthalamic nucleus (Matsumura et al. 1992), pars reticulata of substantia nigra (Sato & Hikosaka 2002), dorsolateral and orbital prefrontal cortex (Tremblay & Schultz 1999), anterior cingulate cortex (ACC) (Niki & Watanabe 1976) and amygdala (Nishijo et al. 1988). Neurons in the ventral striatum show a higher incidence of reward responses and reward expectation activities, compared to caudate and putamen neurons with their larger spectrum of task-related activity. This indicates that subpopulations of striatal neurons process pure reward signals. Orbitofrontal cortex (OFC) responses to rewards and reward-predicting stimuli are related to the motivational value rather than the more sensory properties of reward objects, they then constitute pure reward signals (Critchley & Rolls 1996). Importantly, OFC neurons encode the economic value of rewards for decision-making irrespective of the actual reward objects (Padoa-Schioppa & Assad 2006). In so doing these responses appear to adapt to the current probability distribution of reward values, and a change in this distribution changes the neuronal responses. Such a dependence of responsiveness on a set point corresponds to a basic tenet of prospect theory, indicating that outcomes are valued relative to changing references rather than absolute physical characteristics (Kahneman & Tversky 1984).

However, stimuli and events of different nature can be rewarding. An important proposed property of the reward system is that rewards might be processed based on a common neural currency, signalling the value of the reward on a common neural scale (Sugrue et al. 2005).

From this body of research emerged that dopamine neurons recorded in behaving animals show a rather slow (between 0.1-7 Hz) baseline firing rate characterised by phasic excitatory and inhibitory responses to a number of different types of events. It has been proposed (Montague et al. 1996; Schultz et al. 1997) that the phasic responses elicited by these events can collectively be understood as a reward prediction error similar to the Rescorla-Wagner prediction error, and complies with the principal characteristics of teaching signals of efficient reinforcement models (Sutton & Barto 1998). Reward prediction error signals have long been confirmed in monkey midbrain neurons (Glimcher et al. 2005) as well as in human imaging studies, particularly in putamen (McClure et al. 2003). Signals associated with reward expectation and anticipation have been found in medial prefrontal cortex and in human ventral striatum as well as in the amygdala (Knutson, Fong, et al. 2001; Knutson, Adams, et al. 2001).

Crucially it has been demonstrated that the response to unpredicted primary rewards varies in a monotonic positive fashion with reward magnitude. Prediction errors also covary with reward probability and reflect the discrepancy of the experienced and predicted reward (Fiorillo et al. 2003; Pan et al. 2005; Glimcher et al. 2005).

This last finding is important because the uncertainty of reward can then be tested as risk using different probabilities for the delivery of reward. In the case of only two possible reward outcomes one can then separate expected reward value (linearly increasing from $p=0$ to $p=1$) from risk expressed as variance of the probability distribution of magnitudes (inverted U function with peak at $p=0.5$; see Fig. 1.3). This is in other words the risk-return approach used in finance and presented earlier. There is today growing evidence that this decomposition of risky options into mean and variance is implemented in the brain. Electrophysiological studies first provided proof of a neural differentiation of expected reward and risk (Tobler et al. 2005; Fiorillo et al. 2003). Fiorillo and colleagues (2003) trained two macaque monkeys (Macaca mulatta) in a Pavlovian task (Fig. 1.4) without choice, in which specific visual stimuli indicated the probability of receiving a drop of fruit juice of fixed magnitude and varying probability. Thus, each stimulus indicated a specific probability distribution with two elements, 0 and 0.15 ml. They recorded extracellularly the impulse activity of single dopamine neurons of substantia nigra pars compacta and ventral tegmental area. Not only they observed a widespread activity to the reward-predicting stimuli that increased monotonically with reward probability, thus reflecting quantitative relationships of the known reward prediction error coding (Schultz et al. 1997). Crucially, in about a third of the neurons recorded they observed a separate and more sustained tonic activation (also referred to as ramp effect) during the interval between the stimulus and the reward. This more sustained activity was low for probabilities predicting the occurrence of reward or no reward (probability close to 0 or 1), and high for maximal variance or standard deviation when probability was 0.5 (Fig. 1.5).

Later studies further investigated this dissociation using fMRI in humans and found corresponding phasic and sustained striatal BOLD responses (Dreher et al. 2006; Preuschoff et al. 2006). Importantly, the correlation of a sustained response in dopamine neurons to risk has been also interpreted as the effect of back-propagation of reward prediction errors during learning (Niv et al. 2005). Using an fMRI design that eliminates learning confounds (while controlling for salience and motivation) Preuschoff and colleagues (2006) observed not only striatal activations that scaled with reward probability, but also sustained responses increasing with variance risk. Though this pattern corresponded to the temporal dissociation of mean and variance shown by dopamine neurons, it is worth noting that dissociating phasic and tonic components is more difficult with fMRI due to lower temporal resolution.

We said earlier that reward prediction errors, which capture the discrepancy between current and predicted reward values, are thought to critically serve learning about future reward values (Sutton & Barto 1998). We also said that a similar formal mechanism has been proposed to update the learning of risk, where risk prediction errors would signal the discrepancy between current and predicted risk and update our knowledge about risk (Preuschoff & Bossaerts 2007). In an interesting turn of events, this time physiological evidence of the existence of such a neural signal was first found using neuroimaging in anterior insula and other regions (Preuschoff et al. 2008; d'Acremont et al. 2009; Rudorf et al. 2012) and later using primate single neuron recordings in OFC (O'Neill & Schultz 2010; O'Neill & Schultz 2013).

1.3 Decision making under ambiguity

Knowledge about the probability distribution of possible outcomes can lie anywhere on a continuum, from complete ignorance at one end, through various degrees where outcomes may be known but their probabilities not precisely specified (ambiguity), to pure risk where the full outcome distribution is explicitly specified, to certainty.

We previously saw how pure risk has been widely studied in laboratory experiments using ad hoc designed paradigms for humans and other animals. Such experimental manipulations have been effective in exposing fundamental knowledge about how the brain produces decisions in the face of constant uncertainty. One could argue though that throughout evolution the brain of animals has been exposed mainly to situations of ambiguity where probability distributions of outcomes are not explicitly revealed.

Neoclassical economic analysis assumed that uncertain situations could be reduced to risky situations. So in the absence of information about probabilities, all possible values would be considered equally likely, with the midpoint of the range as the best estimate. Contrary to this assumption, the famous Ellsberg paradox (1961) showed that people distinguish between risky and ambiguous choice options and clearly tend to be ambiguity averse (Camerer & Weber 1992).

The question that arises is then whether ambiguity should be treated separately from risk as is often suggested in economics (Knight 1921) or if ambiguity and risk are two facets of a more general form of uncertainty. Competing theories view risk and ambiguity as two extremes of a continuum of uncertainty or as two distinct forms of uncertainty with separate underlying neural systems. In controlled laboratory settings, ambiguity can be tested quantitatively in situations of uncertainty by withholding parts of information about probabilities.

A number of studies have shown that neural correlates of ambiguity in regions such as posterior parietal cortex, dorsolateral prefrontal cortex, anterior insula and striatum (Hsu et al. 2005; Huettel et al. 2006; Bach et al. 2009) have a distinct representation compared to the neural correlates of pure risk economic gambles (Preuschoff et al. 2008; Tobler et al. 2007; Dreher et al. 2006; Preuschoff et al. 2006). In particular, compared to pure risk, ambiguity elicits higher mean BOLD activity in orbitofrontal cortex (Levy et al. 2010; Hsu et al. 2005), amygdala (Hsu et al. 2005) and in some studies also in parietal cortex (Bach et al. 2011;

Huettel et al. 2006). One interpretation is that these regions may, by this increased activity, signal that information is missing. Taken together, these results suggest some degree of neural separation between risky and ambiguous decision making.

In the next chapter we venture in the domain of social decision making and valuation. There seems to be a clear link between the economic concept of ambiguity and that of social valuation and choice. Primates and humans in particular, throughout their life, navigate a universe whose fabric is social in nature. Uncertainty generated by social stimuli such as faces or voices provide no explicit distribution of probabilities to the decision-maker. In this sense social ambiguity can be thought of as a distinct form of uncertainty compared to pure risk (where probability distributions are known) and pure ambiguity (where probability distributions are partially known).

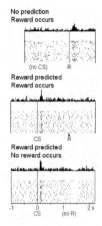

Figure 1.1. Reward prediction error response of single dopamine neuron (from Schultz et al. 1997).

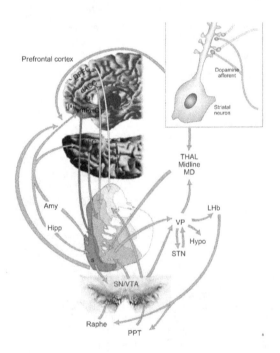

Figure 1.2. Connectivity of dopamine regions with striatum and cortex. Dopamine neurons (bottom) project to the ventral and dorsal striatum and other regions. Together with the striatum, the pallidum and the subthalamic nucleus (STN), the substantia nigra forms the basal ganglia. Abbreviations: VP, ventral pallidum; THAL, thalamus; LHb, lateral habenula; Amy, amygdala; Hipp, hippocampus - adapted from (Daw & Tobler 2014).

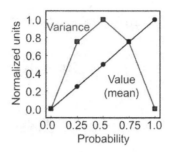

Figure 1.3. Dissociation of mean and variance by variation in probability adapted from (Daw & Tobler 2014).

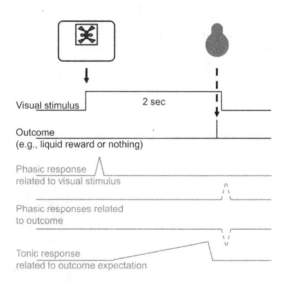

Figure 1.4. Visual stimuli are followed by outcomes with different probabilities or magnitudes. Typical neural responses are shown in red and can correspond to activation increases or decreases - adapted from (Daw & Tobler 2014).

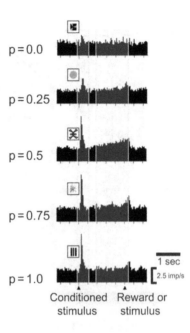

Figure 1.5. Temporal decomposition of value and risk in population of dopamine neurons. Different conditioned stimuli predicted reward (2 s later, right arrowhead) of a given magnitude at the probabilities indicated on the left. Value of stimuli increases with probability and so does phasic response induced by reward-predicting stimuli (left shading). By contrast, variance risk is represented in a sustained response building up to time of outcome (right shading) highest at p=0.5 (from Fiorillo et al. 2003).

2 Neural Basis of Social Valuation under Uncertainty

The previous chapter focused on reward processing, the base of animal motivational decision making. Most of these experimental studies of learning and decision making have examined choices with clearly defined probabilities and outcomes, such as choosing between monetary gambles. The reality for human beings (as well as for other primates) is that we live in highly complex social environments, and most of our decisions are made in the context of social interactions. Our decisions are dependent on the concomitant choices of others. Social neuroscience and in particular the interdisciplinary field of neuroeconomics, in their recent history, have begun to investigate both the psychological and neural correlates of social decisions. Key to this scientific enterprise is, on the one hand, the large body of research that social neuroscience has accumulated on how the brain processes specific social stimuli such as faces, voices, body movement (Todorov et al. 2013; Belin et al. 2000; Peelen & Downing 2007) and social judgments (Lieberman 2007). On the other hand, the more recent neuroeconomic approach, using tasks derived from a branch of experimental economics known as game theory (Lee 2008), has started to unravel the intricate universe of social interaction by exposing both the psychological and neural bases (Fehr & Camerer 2007).

The neuroscientific study of social judgements from the human face offers, thanks to the large amount of literature accumulated, an ideal window into some of the driving forces of social choice. In fact, perception of trust is mainly and immediately communicated through this biological medium. Also, in analogy with the study of non-social reward processing, though social decision making is constrained by complex variables such as trust and fairness, equivalent neural mechanisms underlying value and uncertainty processing can be investigated using strategic games that can formally account for these social variables.

2.1 Neuroscience of social judgements from faces

No other category of social stimuli has been studied as extensively as human faces. This is reflected in the vast amount of research on the cognitive and neural basis of face perception (Calder et al. 2011). Faces convey information about the person identity, mental, and emotional states (Haxby et al. 2001) and influence important social outcomes. A number of studies have shown systematic effects of facial appearance on social interactions (Schlicht et al. 2010; Tingley 2014; Rezlescu et al. 2012). Judgments of competence based on face perception predict the outcomes of important political elections (Olivola & Todorov 2010) and judgments of criminality predict identification of suspects (Flowe & Humphries 2011). Furthermore attractive faces have a reward value (Kampe et al. 2001; Aharon et al. 2001) and can elicit reward prediction error like signals in areas of the reward system in the context of a reinforcement learning task (Bray & O'Doherty 2007).

Human beings are particularly efficient at making face trustworthiness judgments. In a study (Willis & Todorov 2006) that investigated five trait judgments from emotionally neutral faces (likability, trustworthiness, competence, aggressiveness, and attractiveness), the authors found that all five judgments, even if made after extremely short periods of exposure to novel faces (below 100ms), closely agreed with control judgments made in the absence of time constraints. Importantly, the agreement for judgments of trustworthiness was as high as the agreement for judgments of attractiveness. Attractiveness is a property of facial appearance, and it is striking that specific trait judgments such as trustworthiness are processed with same accuracy. Judgments of trustworthiness are highly correlated with other trait judgments (Todorov et al. 2013). These correlations suggest that trustworthiness judgments from faces reflect the general evaluation of the face. In a recent meta-analysis on the social valuation of faces, contrasts showing stronger neural responses to positive (attractive or trustworthy) than to negative (unattractive or untrustworthy) faces were reflected in consistent activations around the nucleus accumbens, medial orbitofrontal cortex (mOFC), ventromedial prefrontal cortex (vmPFC) and right amygdala (Fig. 2.1), (Mende-Siedlecki et al. 2012).

Meta-analyses of fMRI studies consistently identify the amygdala as responsive to faces (Bzdok et al. 2011; Sergerie et al. 2008). In particular they indicate that amygdala plays a key role in the evaluation of face trustworthiness. We know that amygdala is involved in multiple psychological functions (Whalen & Phelps 2009) from learning of fear responses and consolidation of emotional memories (McGaugh 2004), to implicit evaluation of stimuli (Vuilleumier 2005), as well as reward anticipation (Holland & Gallagher 2004). The variety of computational functions of amygdala is such that a long and intriguing anatomical debate is still ongoing, questioning whether or not amygdala can be considered a structural unit. The most radical theory comes from Swanson and collaborators (1998), who proposed the idea that the amygdala does not exist as a structural unit. Instead they argued that what we call amygdala consists of regions that belong to other regions or systems of the brain and that the designation "amygdala" is not necessary. For example, in this scheme, the lateral and basal amygdala is viewed as nuclear extensions of the neocortex (rather than amygdala regions related to the neocortex); the central and medial amygdala are said to be ventral extensions of the striatum, and the cortical nucleus is associated with the olfactory system.

The amygdala is generally thought to respond to emotional stimuli, with a particular emphasis on negative ones (e.g. threatening or fear-related stimuli). A wide range of studies using faces supports this view (Adolphs et al. 1995; Whalen 1998). Some researchers also suggested a model of amygdala as a biological marker of negative attitudes and emotions (Eberhardt et al. 2006). However other neuroimaging studies have reported greater amygdala activation for both positive and negative stimuli compared with neutral stimuli. Pessoa and collaborators (Pessoa & Adolphs 2010) using fMRI showed greater amygdala activation for happy and fearful faces compared with neutral faces. A study with patients with bilateral amygdala damage showed a bias to perceive untrustworthy faces as trustworthy (Adolphs et al. 1998). Also other two functional neuroimaging studies (Winston et al. 2002; Engell et al. 2007) confirmed the involvement of the amygdala in face evaluation on trustworthiness and further showed that faces are spontaneously evaluated on this dimension. These findings suggest that trustworthy faces could evoke a stronger amygdala response than faces in the middle of the trustworthiness dimension. In the context of the present work where non-social and social valuation and uncertainty are compared, a study of particular interest is that from Said and collaborators (2009). They modelled amygdala activation with both linear and nonlinear predictors and found a nonlinear response to face trustworthiness (quadratic concave function) with elevated responses to both extremely trustworthy and untrustworthy faces (Fig. 2.2).

Modelling the amygdala response as a linear function of face trustworthiness would have missed this effect. Consistent with previous findings of linear amygdala activation to perceived trustworthiness (Winston et al. 2002; Engell et al. 2007), the amygdala response was more sensitive to differences at the negative than at the positive end of the trustworthiness dimension. This nonlinear response profile is inconsistent with functional descriptions of the amygdala as a detector of fear or negative stimuli. In fact these results are consistent with the idea that amygdala detects salience and directs attention toward emotionally relevant stimuli (Vuilleumier 2005). We will later discuss, in the context of our first experimental study, an alternative interpretation of these data and suggest a general method to investigate social judgements from faces when these social variables are highly correlated with uncertainty.

2.2 Social decision-making and fairness behavior under uncertainty

Key to the study of social decisions and valuation has been the use of game theory (Von Neumann & Morgenstern 1944), a collection of models that aim to understand situations in which decision-makers interact with one another. This approach offers well-specified models for the investigation of social interaction and exchange (Lee 2008).

In most classical game theoretical analyses, rational, self-interested players are expected to make decisions to reach outcomes known as Nash equilibria (Nash 1950). These are a set of strategies from which no individual players can increase their payoffs by changing their strategies unilaterally. In reality, decision-makers are generally less selfish and strategic than the model predicts and value social factors such as reciprocity and equity (Camerer 2003). One important area of focus has been strategic bargaining and the application of several variants of the ultimatum game, the trust game and the prisoner's dilemma game (Sanfey 2007).

It is well known that fairness behaviour is an important concept in society and that people generally understand what a fair outcome is from an early age (Fehr et al. 2008). Deviations from a fair (equitable) outcome are therefore generally viewed in a negative light. The task used to examine responses to fairness is often the ultimatum game. Two players interact to decide how to divide a sum of money that is given to them. The first player proposes how to divide the sum, and the second player can either accept or reject this proposal. If the second player rejects, neither player receives anything. If the second player accepts, the money is split according to the proposal. If people are motivated purely by self-interest the responder should accept any offer and the proposer should offer the smallest amount. However what normally is observed is something closer to a 50/50 split, and offers lower than 20% of the total amount are rejected about half of the times (Güth et al. 1982). People's choice in the ultimatum game do not conform to the homo economicus model in which decisions are driven only by self-interest, and as we will see later neuroeconomics has begun to clarify the mechanisms underlying these decisions.

Reciprocal exchange is another form of behaviour that involves decision-making between people and is often studied using the prisoner's dilemma game (PDG) and the trust game (we will expand on the latter later). In its classical form the PDG is presented as follows. Two suspects are arrested by the police. The police officers have insufficient evidence for a conviction, and, having separated both prisoners, visit each of them to offer the same deal. If one testifies (defects from the other) for the prosecution against the other and the other remains silent (cooperates with the other), the betrayer goes free and the silent accomplice receives the full 10-year sentence. If both remain silent, both prisoners are sentenced to only six months in jail for a minor charge. If each betrays the other, each receives a five-year sentence. Each prisoner must choose to either betray the other or to remain silent. In this game the payoffs depend on the interaction of the two choices. The largest payoff occurs when one player defects and the other cooperates (this is at the same time the worst outcome for the cooperator). Mutual cooperation gives a modest amount to both the players, whether mutual defection a lesser amount to each. Classical economic models would predict that mutual defection should be the most frequent situation, but again, in most interactions players show more trust than expected with mutual cooperation observed about 50% of the times (Sally 1995).

Classical models of decision-making have largely ignored the influence of emotions on how decisions are made. The nature of emotions has been the subject of debate for entire fields of science. In this context it is useful to refer to emotions as low-level psychological processes engaged by events that elicit strong valenced and stereotyped behavioural responses. This is in contrast with the capacity for controlled processing and the ability to deliberate rationally about long-term consequences of our behaviour. Emotional processes, we know today, involve the activity of a set of structures closely related to the reward-processing system. These regions include the ventromedial prefrontal cortex (vmPFC), orbitofrontal cortex, anterior cingulate cortex, amygdala and insula (Fig. 2.3). Although emotional processes, like other automatic processes, share common neural substrates with controlled processes, it is becoming clear from neuroimaging studies that different types of processes involve distinctive neural components. High-level deliberative processes such as problem solving and planning consistently involve the activity of anterior and dorsolateral regions of the prefrontal cortex (Miller & Cohen 2001). On the other hand automatic processes involve the activity of more posterior cortical structures, as well as subcortical systems. In particular emotional processes seem to engage a set of structures classically referred to as limbic system, which includes reward-processing structures such as the ventral tegmental area, areas of the midbrain to which they project (nucleus accumbens and ventromedial, frontal, orbitofrontal and cingulate cortex), and other important areas such as amygdala and insular cortex (Dalgleish 2004).

The neural mechanisms responsible for deliberation and emotion are clearly closely interrelated, and distinguishing between these could help shed light on many of the most basic patterns uncovered by neuroeconomics. An important study (Sanfey et al. 2003) examining the neural correlates of the ultimatum game using fMRI revealed the role of two key brain regions: the anterior insula and the dorsolateral prefrontal cortex (dlPFC). Activation in these areas has been shown to correlate with emotional and deliberative processing. In particular it has been found that if the insular activation was greater than in the dlPFC participants tended to reject the offer, whereas if the dlPFC activation was greater they tended to accept the offer. This observation provided neural evidence of a two-system account of decision-making (Bechara & Damasio 2005). In a related study (Rilling et al. 2004) the insular area was also active in an iterated prisoner's dilemma game. Subjects with a stronger anterior insular response to unreciprocated cooperation showed a higher frequency of defection. The observation of anterior insula activation is of particular interest as this brain region is also responsive to physically painful (Derbyshire et al. 1997) and disgusting (Calder et al. 2001) stimuli and is involved in mapping physiological states of the body (Singer et al. 2009). Taken together these studies show that anterior insula and associated areas involved in the processing of emotions may play an important role in identifying social interactions as aversive and thus discouraging trust of that partner in the future.

We said earlier that one possible hypothesis about the role of the dlPFC is that unfair offers in the ultimatum game generate an impulse to reject the offer, and that dlPFC activity is involved in controlling this impulse (Sanfey et al. 2003). Therefore dlPFC would be involved in the cognitive control of the emotional impulse associated with fair behaviour. Another plausible hypothesis is that fundamental impulses associated with self-interested behaviour need to be controlled in order to maintain and to implement culture-dependent fairness goals (Henrich et al. 2001). However, both hypotheses are consistent with a dual-system approach (Bechara & Damasio 2005) that stresses the differences between automatic and controlled processes, because both fairness and selfish behaviour may have strong emotional content. To clarify the role of the dlPFC in social exchange, Knock and colleagues used direct stimulation methodologies such as transcranial magnetic stimulation (TMS) (Knoch, Gianotti, et al. 2006; Knoch, Pascual-Leone, et al. 2006; Fecteau et al. 2007; Knoch et al. 2008). They showed that disruption of the right, but not the left, dlPFC by low-frequency repetitive transcranial magnetic stimulation (rTMS) reduces subjects' willingness to reject their partners' intentionally unfair offers during the ultimatum game. In particular, these results show that disruption of the right dlPFC only affects fairness behaviour but nor fairness judgments. This is interesting in light of evidence from perceptual decision making showing opposite laterality effects using rTMS, and linking the mechanism of evidence accumulation to the left dlPFC (Philiastides et al. 2011). Furthermore, patients with right prefrontal lesions are characterised by the inability to behave in normatively appropriate ways, despite the fact that they can judge rationally what should be the appropriate way to behave socially (Damasio 1994). Also the fact that there is no effect of dlPFC disruption in a computer offer condition (in which participants know to be interacting with a computer and not a person) supports the role of the dlPFC in the processing of reciprocity.

2.3 Neural basis of trust under uncertainty

Reciprocal exchange and trust have also been studied extensively in the laboratory using the trust game. This is a method to operationalise trust by quantifying both trustworthiness and the willingness to trust (Berg et al. 1995). Though there are variants of this game, generally a player (the investor) must decide how much of an endowment to invest with a partner (the trustee). Once transferred, this money is multiplied by some factor, and then the trustee has to decide whether to return money to the investor, but, importantly, he might not return anything. If the trustee honours trust and returns money, both players end up with a higher monetary payoff. However, if the trustee abuses trust and keeps the entire amount, the investor takes a loss. The amount of money sent by the investor and the trustee are said to capture trust and trustworthiness respectively. The money sent by the investor captures the willingness to bet that the trustee will reciprocate, which is a risky move. Likewise, the decision to trust is linked with an expectation that the consequences of the decision will be positive for the investor. This form of trust behaviour has been widely studied using one-shot games performed anonymously (Coleman 1990; Berg et al. 1995). Given that investor and trustee interact only once during the game, game theory predicts that a rational and selfish trustee will never honour the trust given by the investor. Consequently, the investor should never place trust in the first place. Despite these clear theoretical predictions, a majority of investors do in fact send some amount of money to the trustee, and this trust is generally reciprocated. A more recent meta-analysis of trust game studies reported trust related behaviours and reciprocity across gender, age, culture, showing that investors send more than half of their initial endowment and trustees reciprocate with more than the amount received (Johnson & Mislin 2011).

The trust game has been used in a number of fMRI studies investigating the neural bases of trust (King-Casas et al. 2005), cooperation (Decety et al. 2004) and reciprocity (Phan et al. 2010; Krueger et al. 2007). Generally these studies report a higher BOLD signal in the medial prefrontal cortex (mPFC) when participants were interacting with a human counterpart compared to a computer (McCabe et al. 2001; Rilling et al. 2002), and when participants decided to trust compared to no trust (McCabe et al. 2001; Krueger et al. 2007; Phan et al. 2010; Delgado et al. 2005; King-Casas et al. 2005).

In a widely cited study King-Casas and colleagues (2005) using the trust game showed neural correlates of social prediction errors, in analogy with what had been found in non-social settings (Schultz et al. 1997). In the study pairs of participants played trust games repeatedly against each other while their brain activity was recorded by two simultaneous fMRI acquisitions (hyperscanning technique; Fig. 2.4). They found that activation in the trustee's caudate was related to how much reciprocity the investor had shown on previous trials. Crucially, this signal gradually shifted in time. In early trials the signal occurred after the investor made his choice, whereas later on, this signal occurred much earlier, before the investor's decision was revealed. Therefore early caudate's response to trustworthy behaviour, at time of outcome, shifted to the time of the decision, showing evidence of reward prediction errors common to model-based reinforcement learning systems (Sutton & Barto 1998), but in the context of a social exchange. Other studies have shown that activity in the striatum may register social prediction errors to guide decisions about reciprocity (Rilling et al. 2002). Also striatal prediction errors and behavioural learning during the outcome of trust decisions can be suppressed when information about the opponents' trustworthiness is presented, suggesting that strong priors can overrule the importance of new information gathered during single games (Fouragnan et al. 2013).

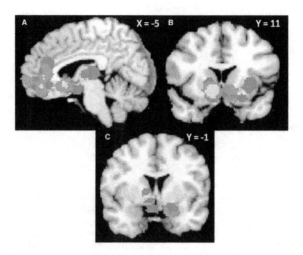

Figure 2.1. Meta-analysis of social valuation of faces. Figure shows consistently activated areas across positive evaluations, including vmPFC (A), left caudate/nucleus accumbens extending into mOFC (A and B), and right amygdala (C) (adapted from Mende-Siedlecki et al. 2012).

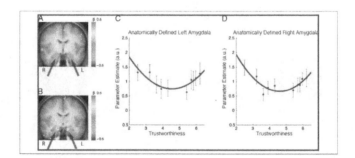

Figure 2.2. Amygdala non-linear response to trustworthiness. (A) Coronal view, showing small clusters in both amygdalae with a linear response to trustworthiness. (B) Coronal slice showing significant clusters with quadratic effects of trustworthiness. (C and D) Results of a separate analysis on the anatomically defined left and right amygdala. Individual faces were binned into groups of four and collapsed across spatial frequency. The average trustworthiness rating of each bin is plotted against the average amygdala response, and a second-order polynomial with a linear term is fit to the plot. Error bars represent the SEM (from Said et al. 2009).

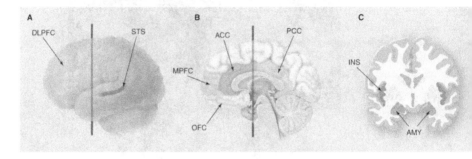

Figure 2.3. Brain areas commonly activated in social decision-making studies. (A) The lateral view shows the location of the dorsolateral prefrontal cortex (DLPFC) and superior temporal sulcus (STS). (B) The sagittal section shows the location of the anterior cingulate cortex (ACC), medial prefrontal cortex (MPFC), orbitofrontal cortex (OFC), and posterior cingulate cortex (PCC). (C) The coronal section shows the location of the insula (INS) and amygdala (AMY) (from Sanfey 2007).

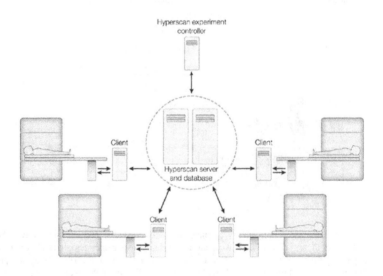

Figure 2.4. Hyperscanning fMRI setup. Such a setup allows simultaneous functional neuroimaging of subjects as they interact with each other. The data collected by each functional magnetic image is passed, through a client, to a hyperscan server and database, which is regulated by an experiment controller (from Casebeer 2003).

3 Toward an Integration of Social and Non-Social Risky Decision Making

In the past two chapters we have introduced some key findings in the study of the neural underpinnings of social and non-social forms of decision making under uncertainty. This overview exposed areas of convergence (social and non-social decision-making engage similar regions of the reward system), as well as areas of divergence (some brain structures are mainly engaged in social settings or when social stimuli like faces are perceived). Recently a similar conceptual framework has been explicitly proposed in order to illustrate how neural value representations underlying social decisions could relate to those driving non-social choices (Ruff & Fehr 2014). In this framework areas of convergence are grouped under the "extended common currency schema", where identical neural processes are thought to assign motivational value to social and non-social factors. Similarly, areas of divergence are grouped under the "social valuation specific schema", where social rewards are thought to be processed in a dedicated neural circuitry that evolved specifically to deal with interactions with others (Fig. 3.1).

The first of these two schemas is the natural extension to the social domain of the idea of a common neural scale (common currency) emerging from a large number of studies assessing the reward properties of choice options in the non-social domain (Rangel et al. 2008; Kable & Glimcher 2009). In light of the evidence in favour of neural activity correlated mainly with social factors, this schema postulates that though both domains of choice induce similar activity in the brain value system, these shared value representations change their functional connectivity with other, domain-specific brain regions. The second schema is less inclusive and postulates that social and non-social value signals are implemented in different spatial patterns of brain activity. Owing to the evidence in favour of a common neural scale for a variety of choice options (Rangel et al. 2008), this schema predicts that these two spatially distinct circuitries derive social values using types of neural computations similar to those used by the neurons that encode non-social value representations.

With two explicit frameworks that make specific predictions, scientists can interpret the results of a fast growing literature using specific lenses. This in turn can help establish which of the two schemas better represents our current understanding of the neurobiology of social and non-social decisions.

Using the lens provided by the extended common currency schema, one would for instance note that several aspects of direct social interactions (like receiving approval and being rejected) have been linked to neural activity in brain structures involved in encoding non-social rewards (Izuma et al. 2008; Zink et al. 2008; Spreckelmeyer et al. 2009; Sescousse et al. 2010; Rademacher et al. 2010). In particular in one of these studies participants completed a non-social gambling task (in which monetary rewards were the outcome) and a social reward task (in which others' positive evaluations of the participant's personality constituted the reward). Despite the different structure of the social and non-social tasks, social and monetary rewards were reflected in comparable BOLD activations in the ventral striatum (Izuma et al. 2008).

Likewise, under the lens of the social valuation specific schema would fall several studies showing that during social interactions, prediction error computations can be observed in regions outside the classic reward system. For instance, the posterior temporal sulcus can encode prediction errors related to a mismatch in romantic interest from an interaction partner (Cooper et al. 2014) or the credibility of a confederate's advice (Behrens et al. 2008). Importantly, in the latter, these social reward prediction errors occurred in parallel to financial-reward prediction errors expressed in the ventral striatum.

A more in depth analysis of studies involving experienced value coding of social rewards, computation of anticipated value associated with a given social choice and prediction-error-like neural signals during social learning, reveals the involvement of neural processes in the ventral striatum, vmPFC, amygdala and insula. This is what is normally identified in the context of non-social decision making and therefore speaks clearly in favour of the extended common currency schema (Ruff & Fehr 2014). It is also true that standard fMRI does not provide enough spatial resolution to clarify whether the overlapping areas found for social and non-social decisions actually recruit distinct neural populations (Logothetis 2008). A partial answer to this problem might come from single neuron recording studies in non-human primates that have identified different types of neurons in the striatum selectively encoding social versus non-social aspects of rewards. In one study neurons in the striatum have been found to respond to social (images of conspecifics) or non-social (juice) rewards (Klein &

Platt 2013). Another study identified neurons of the striatum involved in signalling either when a reward was given or when this reward was due to the action of the monkey or a conspecific (Báez-Mendoza et al. 2013). Therefore it seems as though enhancing spatial resolution can bring crucial evidence in favour of the social valuation specific schema.

It is also worth considering that the main difference in neural processing during social and non-social decisions might not consist in local value computations but rather in separate anatomical neural regions providing the information on which the measured computations are based. Consistent with this view, several studies investigating social decisions report responses correlated with the construction of uniquely social values in regions outside the classic valuation circuitry such as the dlPFC (Baumgartner et al. 2011), temporo parietal junction (Carter et al. 2012) and dmPFC (Nicolle et al. 2012). This possibility has been also tested with connectivity analyses (Behrens et al. 2008; Baumgartner et al. 2011).

Some crucial observations emerge from this brief account. Although it is possible to distinguish results favouring one or the other schema, only few of these studies have been designed to directly compare activity patterns elicited by social outcomes with those due to non-social financial rewards. In particular we identified four aspects that similar studies would need to address: (a) creating experimental paradigms where direct comparison of social and non-social value and uncertainty is made within the same experiment, possibly using a within subject design; (b) using designs that make possible a direct comparison of social and non-social variables based on a comparable scale; (c) using connectivity analyses to establish by direct comparison how social versus non-social decisions might change patterns of connectivity; (d) and finally, when assessing overlap between social and non-social factors in a region of interest (and to avoid reverse inference), the same clusters found for one domain (e.g. non-social) might be used as regions of interest to directly test convergence or divergence from a common currency model in the other domain (e.g. social).

We will further discuss these points in the context of our experimental studies presented later.

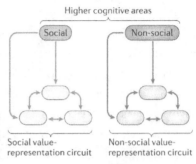

a Extended common currency schema   **b** Social-valuation-specific schema

Figure 3.1. Two schemas for neural value computation in social versus non-social decision making.
The two competing schemas illustrate how the brain might determine the value of social and non-social factors during decision making. A) The extended common currency schema assumes that a single neural circuit (shown in purple) determines the motivational significance of both social and non-social events. The activity of this circuit represents the integrated value of all factors that are relevant for a choice; however, the perceptual and cognitive information that is relevant for these unified value computations might differ between social and non-social choices and might be provided by distinct domain-specific brain areas (shown in blue and red, respectively). B) In the social valuation specific schema, neural valuation of social and non-social factors engages neural processes that follow similar computational principles but are implemented in distinct neuronal populations that are specialised for each type of information. These specialised neurons may be located in different areas (shown in light blue and light red, respectively) or in close proximity within a value-processing brain region (from Ruff & Fehr 2014).

4 Predictive Coding, Perceptual and Motivational Prediction Errors

In the first chapter we saw that the concepts of prediction and prediction error are central in models of reward learning and motivational decision-making (Schultz et al. 1997; Schultz 2013; Sutton & Barto 1998). Although the two fields might seem distantly related to each other, the same concepts of prediction and predictor errors are key in the study of the perceptual system, and are employed in prominent models that show how prior expectations shape perception (Rao & Ballard 1999; Lee & Mumford 2003). A wealth of experiments in these fields of study has led to theories suggesting that coding of prediction errors does indeed reflect a general neural coding strategy throughout the brain (Friston 2005; Clark 2013).

We said earlier that a prediction error can be defined as the mismatch between a prior expectation and what actually reality presents to the subject. It is generally thought that prediction errors are based on a model of the world in part hard-wired in the structure of neural circuits and in part derived from statistical regularities in the sensory inputs (den Ouden et al. 2012). Two broad categories of prediction error have been identified in the brain: perceptual prediction errors (known also as unsigned) and motivational prediction errors (known also as signed).

Perceptual prediction errors signal the degree of surprise with respect to a particular outcome (see Table 4.1). These signals can be dissociated from related concepts like adaptation and stimulus-driven attention. Experiments using omission paradigms (where neural responses to a predicted but withheld event are measured), have shown a robust cortical response to such surprising stimulus omissions in different sensory cortical areas (den Ouden et al. 2009; Todorovic et al. 2011; Kok et al. 2012). These brain responses to surprising omissions cannot be interpreted in terms of stimulus adaptation, since there is no physical stimulus presented. Perceptual prediction errors have been reported not only within, but also between sensory modalities. Experiments in audiovisual speech perception, report that incongruence between the visual (lip movements) and auditory (speech) stimuli increased neural activity in the superior temporal sulcus. Also, in line with predictive coding accounts, the more predictive a visual stimulus was, the stronger the response in superior temporal sulcus was when this prediction had been violated (Arnal et al. 2009). It is important to note that perceptual predictor errors do not merely signal surprise, as they are linked to a particular representation or prediction. In line with this view studies using the omission paradigm have shown that the activity pattern of omissions contains information about the identity of the absent stimulus (Peelen & Kastner 2011).

Compared to perceptual prediction errors, motivational prediction errors signal not only the size of the mismatch between the prior model of the world and the encountered reality. These signals are said to be signed, meaning that they also signal the valence of the mismatch: not only whether the outcome was surprising, but also whether it was better or worse than expected (in a survival and biological sense). We presented earlier the seminal studies from Schultz and colleagues showing that the firing pattern of phasic dopamine neurons in the macaque ventral tegmental area (VTA) reflects what came to be known as reward prediction error (Romo & Schultz 1990; Mirenowicz & Schultz 1994; Schultz et al. 1997).

More recently evidence has emerged indicating that specialised neuronal populations might reflect punishment prediction errors. In one study neurons in the primate lateral habenula showed increased activity after an unexpected punishment, and decreased activity after an unexpected reward (Matsumoto & Hikosaka 2007). Similar punishment predictor errors have been observed in the VTA (Cohen et al. 2012). Also, similar signals have been reported using fMRI in the human striatum (Seymour et al. 2007) and in the amygdala (Yacubian et al. 2007).

Recent predictive coding models postulates that the brain builds a generative model of how causes in the world elicit sensory inputs (Spratling 2008; Rao & Ballard 1999; Friston 2005). Such models can be inverted to recognise the causes of these inputs. It is thought that each level of the processing hierarchy receives bottom-up sensory input from the level below and top-down predictions from the level above. In this context prediction errors are the difference between the true and estimated probability distribution of the causes. It follows that one fundamental biological function of this system consists in minimising the constant flow of prediction errors arising at all levels of the hierarchy. It has been proposed that, at the cellular level, this is achieved by adjusting the connection strengths through synaptic plasticity (Friston 2005). These models consider the cortical column as the basic computational module and postulates the existence of separate prediction and prediction error units within each cortical column (nonetheless the model also applies to subcortical structures; Fig. 4.1). Connections between prediction and prediction error units happen both within and between columns. There is indeed some experimental evidence showing that higher processing stages create internal models on the basis of learned associations and current context, and convey predicted input to the next lower level of the cortical hierarchy via feedback (Clark 2013). Studies show that correctly predicted bottom-up signals are cancelled from further processing (Rao & Ballard 1999), or attenuated (Alink et al. 2010; Fang et al. 2008). Also, the activation to a stimulus is reduced when it is predictable by its recent past. For instance image sequences in natural movies are more predictable and lead to reduced activation of inferior temporal cortical neurons (Meyer & Olson 2011; Perrett et al. 2009) and reduction in neuronal response in V1 (Kim et al. 2012).

Different biologically plausible hierarchical models have been proposed for both cortical and subcortical systems, postulating the existence of specialised prediction and prediction error units (den Ouden et al. 2012).

In early visual cortex prediction errors might be generated in the granular layer (e.g. L4) of a cortical column, by subtracting the prediction response of the agranular layers from the input provided by lower levels (Fig. 4.1). When a large prediction error occurs two events are expected. The new updated prediction will be sent forward as input to higher cortical areas (via superficial layers). At the same time the same prediction will be sent backward to update predictions in lower areas (via deep layers).

At the subcortical level a similar integration of feedback predictions and feedforward inputs is thought to give rise to prediction errors. Using optogenetic techniques in mice, Cohen and colleagues (2012) exposed a crucial biological passage predicted by theoretical models (Schultz et al. 1997). The study revealed that a top-down inhibitory input on the dopaminergic neurons in the VTA in proportion to the expected reward is present during the delay between a predictive cue and the outcome. It is also interesting to note that in the same study GABAergic (inhibitory) neurons showed persistent activity during the delay between a reward-predicting cue and the outcome. These neurons are thought to provide an inhibitory influence that counteracts the driving excitatory input from primary rewards when the reward is expected. In turn these GABAergic neurons receive feedback from the higher and lower levels in the hierarchy (prefrontal and subcortical inputs), which could relay the reward prediction signals generated by the stimuli (Takahashi et al. 2011; Matsumoto & Hikosaka 2007).

What emerges from these studies is a general mechanism that provides precise working hypotheses to test whether such a unified model is actually reflected in the biology of the brain. As more evidence accumulates on the key biological aspects underlying predictive coding models, it will also become more clear how social and non-social forms of prediction errors are implemented and whether the same neural populations are involved (as predicted by the extended common currency schema outlined in the second chapter). Another open question is whether signed and unsigned prediction errors are to be found at all levels of the brain hierarchy. Unsigned prediction errors have been found also in subcortical regions previously thought to code only motivational prediction errors such as the primate midbrain (Matsumoto & Hikosaka 2009), the human striatum (Zink et al. 2003; den Ouden et al. 2010) and VTA (Bunzeck & Düzel 2006). Although there is less evidence, recently a number of studies showed signed prediction errors in cortical regions: in orbitofrontal cortex (Takahashi et al. 2009; O'Neill & Schultz 2013; O'Neill & Schultz 2010), the insular cortex (Pessiglione et al. 2006; Preuschoff et al. 2008), and in the medial prefrontal cortex (Matsumoto & Hikosaka 2007). Interestingly it is unclear whether activity in early visual areas can reflect signed prediction errors through perhaps feedback mechanisms (Petro et al. 2014). A number of animal studies indicate that reward modulates the representation of features in primary visual area V1. For instance, V1 neurons in the rat have been shown to signal value (Shuler & Bear 2006), and a similar observation has been made in the macaque V1 (Stănişor et al. 2013). Also in humans there is evidence that economic value can influence activation levels within the early visual cortex, including V1 area, even in the absence of saccadic responses (Serences 2008; Serences & Saproo 2010). Therefore studies combining methodologies employed in reinforcement learning experiments (e.g. game theory) as well as paradigms typical of vision neuroscience (e.g. retinotopic techniques) are needed in order to establish whether motivational prediction errors are reflected in primary visual areas.

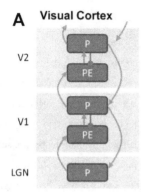
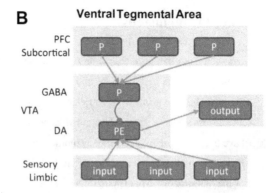

Figure 4.1. A cortical and a subcortical example of hierarchical model. (A) Generation of prediction errors within a cortical ensemble. Prediction errors (PE) are generated by mismatch between predictions (P, in agranular layers, inhibitory) and input (originating from L2/3 from lower unit, arriving in L4, excitatory). The PE unit therefore reflects the difference between input and prediction, and activity in prediction units will be updated to minimise this discrepancy. Predictions (P) are both sent forward as input to a hierarchically higher level and backward to update predictions at a lower level. (B) Generation of predictor errors within VTA (ventral tegmental area). VTA GABAergic neurons exert an inhibitory influence that counteracts the driving excitatory input from primary rewards when the reward is expected (adapted from den Ouden et al. 2012).

Table 4.1

Perceptual vs Motivational Prediction Errors

When our perceptual system produces some inference on some particular aspect of the world, though the outcome can be more or less surprising, at this level it will not be labelled as better or worse than expected. These types of prediction errors, which do not reflect the valence of the outcome but simply the surprise engendered by this outcome, are often referred to as unsigned prediction errors (or perceptual prediction errors; den Ouden et al. 2012). However, we also know that in order to learn and use prediction errors to guide motivational behaviour, not only the size but also the valence (i.e. sign) of the prediction error is of relevance. At this level of the neural hierarchy the prediction error therefore has to reflect also whether an outcome was better or worse than expected. We refer to this type as motivational prediction error.

Part I Conclusions

Drawing from the large collection of experimental evidence investigating the neural basis of non-social forms of decision making, neuroeconomics has been able to apply similar methodologies to uncover the intricate world of social interaction, value and uncertainty. In an attempt to systematise the fast growing body of experimental research, two main theories have been proposed: the extended common currency and the social valuation specific schema. From this synthesis emerges that often it is difficult to attribute the findings of a study to one or the other theory. This is due to the fact that only few studies to date have been designed to directly compare social and non-social forms of decision making under uncertainty.

Combining research and ideas from neurophysiology, social and visual neuroscience, economics and finance, we used behavioural and fMRI techniques in humans to test the following hypotheses:

a) Social uncertainty is reflected in largely similar regions coding for non-social reward and risk prediction errors (in line with extended common currency schema).

b) A direct test of clusters coding for non-social reward prediction errors would also reflect the same neural profile when coding comparable degrees of social uncertainty.

c) A direct test of clusters coding for non-social risk prediction errors would also reflect the same neural profile when coding comparable degrees of social uncertainty.

d) Using connectivity analyses, a direct comparison between social versus non-social outcome anticipation would reveal similar patterns of functional connectivity.

e) Clusters of anterior insula reflecting non-social risk prediction errors at outcome delivery also reflect social outcome prediction errors as well as fairness differentiation.

d) Functionally defined V1 visual areas reflect social as well as non-social motivational prediction errors.

The next chapters will be devoted to exploring these hypotheses and discussing the experimental findings in relation to the literature, as well as indicating new avenues of investigation.

II Neural Systems Responding to Social and Non-Social Uncertainty in Human Decision Making

Part II Overview

Chapter 5 focuses on modulations of social and non-social uncertainty during outcome anticipation. Chapter 6 focuses on modulations of social and non-social uncertainty at outcome delivery, showing how coding of fairness is related to outcome prediction errors and monetary utility maximisation. Chapter 7 focuses on modulation of social and non-social uncertainty during outcome anticipation in primary visual area V1 using retinotopic mapping techniques.

5 Neural Differentiation of Social and Non-Social Motivational Prediction Errors

5.1 Introduction

Our decisions are rarely free from social influences. In fact most decisions are related to other members of the species, be it taking into account social judgements, deciding for others or together with them. Social interaction permeates the life of people, their individual and collective history and, arguably, anything human culture has ever produced as a whole. The social and biological sciences have studied this subject from different angles that can be directly or indirectly related to social choice. In essence social interaction can be seen as a sophisticated form of species-specific decision making. As such it is plausible to hypothesise that the human brain evolved mechanisms specifically dedicated to making social and non-social type of choices.

Traditionally social and non-social neural mechanisms affecting choice have been investigated using different approaches. A wealth of studies have revealed brain regions specialised for the perception of social stimuli such as faces, voices or bodies (Todorov et al. 2013; Belin et al. 2000; Peelen & Downing 2007), or representing the intentions and emotions of other people (Coricelli & Nagel 2009; Coricelli & Rustichini 2010), with only few focussing on reward uncertainty and the decision making value of them (Singer et al. 2004; Aharon et al. 2001; Kampe et al. 2001; Bray & O'Doherty 2007; Fouragnan et al. 2013). By contrast, researchers focusing on the reward and uncertainty properties of non-social choice options have exposed several brain regions acting as a valuation system (Philiastides 2010; Rangel et al. 2008; Kable & Glimcher 2009) and coding for expected reward and risk (Preuschoff et al. 2006; Preuschoff et al. 2008; Schultz et al. 2008; Schultz 2013). However only few studies have directly compared brain activity related to social outcomes with that produced by non-social rewards (Lauharatanahirun et al. 2012; Izuma et al. 2008; Zink et al. 2008; Spreckelmeyer et al. 2009; Sescousse et al. 2010; Rademacher et al. 2010).

Recently, two main theories have been proposed to explain how the brain might encode uncertainty representations underlying social and non-social choices (Ruff & Fehr 2014). One theory assumes that the brain dedicates largely separate networks for encoding social and non-social forms of uncertainty and for assigning value to different choice alternatives. In contrast, a second theory proposes that the same network processes the different forms of uncertainty and converts the values associated with different choice alternatives into a "common currency" (inputs may come from different brain areas that compute information related to social or non-social choice). Importantly, not only the anatomy of the neural circuitries related to social and non-social uncertainty remains unclear, but also the specific type of computations reflected in the neural profile of uncertainty processing. In fact one can hypothesise that within each of these two theories the neural form that uncertainty processing takes for social and non-social situations can be identical or distinct.

One way to test these hypotheses is to find experimental paradigms where social and non-social decision making and the underlying neural dynamics can be directly compared. An example in the context of value processing is given by Izuma and colleagues (2008). They directly compared neural responses to receiving money versus social praise using functional MRI. They found evidence of substantial overlap between the neural representation of monetary and social reward. In particular, the left putamen and caudate nucleus showed greater activity in response to both higher monetary payoffs and more positive evaluations of the self. This particular case supports the common currency theory in the context of value processing.

Advances in behavioural economics, social and computational neuroscience offer a principled approach to probing the mechanistic details underlying social and non-social decision making under uncertainty (Rangel et al. 2008; Behrens et al. 2008; Ruff & Fehr 2014). Decision making models typically comprise a cascade of different processes: the choice phase, where decision alternatives are evaluated and compared to guide action; the outcome anticipation and outcome delivery phases, where expected reward and risk signals associated with that outcome are computed. Studies comparing social and non-social decision making have mainly focused on the processing of valuation (Ruff & Fehr 2014). Here we will directly compare the neural representation of expected reward and risk in social and non-social situations during the outcome anticipation phase using gambling games.

Decision makers update their representation of the uncertainty associated with different decision alternatives as a function of the information they receive (Glimcher 2011).

Recently it has been shown that during outcome anticipation two types of neural signals, namely the reward prediction error (RePE) and risk prediction error (RiPE) respectively, might be updated every time decision makers receive novel information related to anticipated rewards as these unfold over time (Preuschoff et al. 2006; Preuschoff et al. 2008). In general terms, the RePE is the mismatch between the expected and actual (received) rewards, whereas the RiPE can be thought of as the "mistake" the brain makes in predicting the size of the RePE. Quantitative models of reward processing using a reinforcement learning framework - also known as Temporal Difference (TD) models in the neuroscientific literature (Niv & Schoenbaum 2008) - posit that RePE signals are used to update values associated with potential choices (Sutton & Barto 1998). More recently, a complementary feature of this framework has integrated a formulation of risk from financial theory - also known as Mean-Variance model (Markowitz 1952) - such that RiPE signals are also used to update future estimates of risk and consequently learning of choice values (Bossaerts 2009; Preuschoff & Bossaerts 2007; d'Acremont et al. 2009). Recent experiments using the latter formulation showed that the mean term reflects neural correlates of RePE signals that vary linearly along the full reward probability range (when reward magnitude is kept constant). In contrast the variance term, the mean squared deviation from the expected outcome, reflected RiPE signals that vary quadratically along the full reward probability range (i.e. U-shaped response profile) (Preuschoff et al. 2006; Preuschoff et al. 2008). Crucially, in this formulation RePE and RiPE signals are orthogonal and can therefore be de-coupled using neuroimaging techniques.

Previous studies examining outcome anticipation have shown how RePEs and RiPEs are reflected in the risk and reward circuitry during non-social pure risk economic gambles (Christopoulos et al. 2009; Rudorf et al. 2012; Preuschoff et al. 2006; Preuschoff et al. 2008; Pessiglione et al. 2006; Schultz et al. 2008). However, currently little is known about (a) whether activity in the human brain reflects RePE and RiPE when processing different degrees of social uncertainty, (b) whether or not social and non-social uncertainty is processed by the same neural network (common currency theory), (c) and whether the underlying neural computations within common brain regions are reflected in similar or different activation profiles (common neural scale).

To date only few studies have attempted to compare brain activation patterns related to social versus non-social decision outcomes. One important difference between the tasks employed to investigate one or the other is that risk and expected reward can be directly computed only in non-social economic games. Thus one crucial aspect of our experiment is the creation of parametric stimuli so that their experimental features vary along comparable scales in both the social and non-social domain. Such a comparable scale can be grounded on a formal definition of uncertainty. The two important features of a stimulus representing a decision alternative are its value and associated probability and their product formally predicts optimal decision making (Von Neumann & Morgenstern 1944). Consequently one can vary the degree of value or probability and measure whether the different brain activation patterns reflect fundamentally different computations for social and non-social types of uncertainty. Given our research focus on the neural dynamics of risk and reward uncertainty we manipulated probability while keeping value constant. We therefore devised a method to match non-social and social stimuli such that their reward magnitudes remained constant and reward uncertainty changed linearly (RePE) and quadratically (RiPE) in the probability of winning a gamble.

In this process we attributed an explicit (non-social domain) or implicit (social domain) reward probability to each stimulus that varied linearly within each domain (reward magnitude remained constant across domains). In the non-social domain, stimuli were associated with an exact reward probability (pure risk from 0 to 100%) and participants played card games (Preuschoff et al. 2006). In the social domain, we used degrees of face trustworthiness (our social independent variable), on a continuum between untrustworthy and trustworthy, to modulate social uncertainty while participants played trust games (Berg et al. 1995).

To create a subject-specific one-to-one mapping between face trustworthiness and pure risk probabilities, we conducted a preliminary behavioural study where participants engaged in a series of one-shot trust games. In each game, subjects were presented with a different trustee's face and were asked to indicate the likelihood (in the range 0 to 100%) of receiving a fixed share of an initial endowment entrusted to that individual. This indirect measure of perceived trustworthiness served as our economic indicator of implicit probability associated with a particular face. Note that the advantage of using one-shot trust games (rather than a direct trustworthiness rating of faces) is that trustworthiness judgments are the product of an economic decision as in our experimental paradigm (see Methods).

Subsequently, we used these parametric stimuli in a fMRI study where participants played social trust games and non-social card games. This design ensured that expected reward and risk associated with either a social or non-social gamble were comparable, thus allowing to look for common or distinct neural signatures reflecting equivalent changes in risk and reward uncertainty.

We formed two hypotheses. First, we hypothesised that largely similar brain regions would represent expected reward and risk in the social and non-social domain. Second, we hypothesised to observe a similar response profile to social uncertainty within regions known to respond to different degrees of non-social uncertainty.

5.2 Material and Methods

This methods section describes procedures and analyses that support the results presented in this chapter focusing on outcome anticipation. It also presents procedures and analysis in common with chapters 6 and 7. Methods specific to these chapters will be introduced in their respective methods sections.

5.2.1 Participants

A total of 21 healthy participants (11 females, 10 males; mean age, 26.6 years, ±4.82 SD) took part in the study. All participants gave full informed consent to participate in the study. The study was approved by the University of Glasgow Ethics Review Committee.

5.2.2 Experimental task

The experimental task for both card and trust games had three key steps outlined in Figure 5.1. Both tasks can be thought of as betting on the outcome of a coin toss with an intermediate step revealing that the coin was not truly fair.

At the beginning of the trial participants were told that there is a 50/50 chance for each of 2 outcomes. They placed their bet based on this information and received a reward of 50 pence if their choice matched the actual outcome. At step 2 they gained information regarding the likelihood of the two outcomes (e.g. they learnt that the coin is unfair either increasing or decreasing their probability of receiving the reward). The third step was to expose the actual outcome. We included one final step to check their understanding of the trial outcome by asking them to indicate whether they thought they won or lost on each trial (a penalty of 25 pence was applied to incorrect responses).

Critically, these steps are associated with updating uncertainty and, with such updates, expected value and risk prediction error. The experiment was designed so that the updating process had the same structure in a non-social (card game) and social (trust game) context. This type of design allowed us to test whether the activity in the decision circuitry believed to underlie the integration of risk and value is common in these two contexts. We now describe in more detail the procedure for the non-social task (card betting game, CG) and social task (trust betting game, TG).

Card Betting Game. In the card game participants bet on whether the second of two cards consecutively drawn from a deck of 10 would be higher or lower than the first. They chose higher or lower before the first card was revealed. At this point, the objective probability of winning or losing for either choice is 0.5 and expected value is 0.5x50 (50p was at stake on each trial). Four seconds after making this choice, the first card was revealed and shown for 250ms. This information allowed the participant to update risk and expected value. For example, if they bet the second card would be lower than the first and the first card is a 2, they update their probability of winning to 1/9 (sampling without replacement so each trial resulted in a win or loss). After the first card was revealed, there was then an inter-stimulus interval (ISI) of about 7.5 seconds (fixation mark on screen) before the second card was revealed (shown for 250 ms) where the participants learned the actual outcome and could determine whether they won or lost on that trial. After a second ISI of about 7.5 seconds participants were asked to indicate whether they won or lost on that trial. The next trial with a fresh deck of ten cards began immediately after.

Importantly reward and risk parameters, which are correlated with activity in decision circuitry regions (Preuschoff et al. 2006; Schultz et al. 2008; Preuschoff et al. 2008), vary with reward probability as the first card is revealed and update their value once the second card reveals the outcome. After revelation of the first card the initial (constant) prediction of reward at time of bet is updated and results in a reward prediction error (RePE1). Likewise, the initial (constant) prediction risk is updated and results in a risk prediction error (RiPE1). Before the second card is revealed a new reward and risk prediction signal is generated. And finally at outcome revelation the previous reward and risk predictions are updated and result in a new reward and risk prediction error (RePE2 and RiPE2; see also Appendix I for a more comprehensive mathematical illustration of the reward and risk parameters).

Trust betting game. In a typical trust game, the investor gives a trustee some money. The money is doubled and the trustee decides how much to return to the investor. In our experiment, we described this game to participants but their task was to bet on whether the trustee would return a fixed share of the reward or nothing. This share was fixed at 50% of the sum passed on to the trustee as this is what generally constitutes a fair return as opposed to the unfair 0% (Fehr & Krajbich 2014). In essence this is thus the dictator game and could have been framed as such (i.e. will the person share a sum of money they have received with you). We framed the game as a trust game as it involves exchange and trust, in agreement with the crucial experimental manipulation (face trustworthiness).

The trust game followed a similar risk and timing structure as that of the card game. The participant chose in one shot games whether a randomly selected trustee would share or not share at the beginning of the trial when there was a 0.5 chance of either outcome (trustee shared or didn't share). The participant was then shown the face of the trustee. These faces were selected on the basis of a behavioural study described below to elicit reliably different levels of trustworthiness judgments (from very trustworthy to very untrustworthy). So, on a given trial if the person bet that the trustee would share and was shown a face they judged as untrustworthy, they could update their probability of winning to be less than 0.5 - similar to updating after the first card was revealed in the card task. After seeing the face of the trustee for 250 ms and an ISI of about 7.5 seconds as in the card game, the actual outcome was indicated by a red (meaning that the trustee did not share) or green (trustee shared) square. As in the card game, the participant was then asked to indicate whether they thought they won or lost as in the card game.

Figure 5.1 shows the structure of the trust game in parallel with the card game. Trial sequences were pseudo-randomized. Each participant played 4 sessions with a total of 120 trials (60 card games and 60 trust games). They started off each session with an initial balance of £15. To avoid wealth effects (Rudorf et al. 2012) participants knew that the overall outcome of only one of the four runs randomly chosen would constitute their bonus gain on top of their basic pay of £6 per hour.

One important difference between the trust and card game is that risk and expected reward can be objectively computed only in the latter. However, the trust betting game can be equated with the card game as long as we have a set of faces that could be ranked from 1 (very untrustworthy and will never share) to 10 (very trustworthy and will always share) on an integer scale. Thus we can closely approximate the risk structure of the card game in the trust betting game with the appropriate set of face stimuli. We used the following procedure to select the set of face stimuli for the experiment.

5.2.3 Behavioural study to establish the set of faces used to represent trustees

To establish the set of faces for the trust betting game, participants first ran in a behaviour-only version of the trust betting game that allowed us to infer their trustworthiness judgments on 160 candidate faces (80 female and 80 male selected from a face database collected by the University of Glasgow). Faces covered a wide range in terms of age and ethnic background could vary as they represented local population (Glasgow, UK). In both the behavioural and fMRI studies, the face images were equated for luminance and amplitude spectrum with respect to the spatial frequency content of the images. This minimised the potential effect differences in early visual processing on the areas of interest in the fMRI study. All 160 faces were assessed by each participant in the study.

In this version of the trust game participants were to place a bet on whether the trustee would return a fixed share of money or nothing (like in the fMRI version of the game). They were told that an image of a person whose responses were pre-recorded would be shown after they made their choice ("will share" or "will not share"). After they placed a bet, one of the 160 faces was selected at random and shown for 250ms. Participants were then asked to indicate what chance they had of winning on that trial (starting from 0 with 10% increments until 100%). This subjective probability assessment served as our indicator for the perceived trustworthiness of a given face.

To understand this scoring of the face trustworthiness using this task, consider some examples. If they bet that the trustee would share and the face shown appeared trustworthy, we assumed that they would put a high percentage on their chance of winning. This face was then scored as trustworthy for that observer. Similarly, if they bet that the trustee would not share and then indicated that their chances of winning were low, that face would also be given a high trustworthiness rating for that observer. If they indicated that there was still a 50/50 or near 50/50 chance of winning, that face was assigned as ambiguous for that participant.

Running the experiment this way served to give an economic indicator for the individual's trustworthiness judgments and gave each participant practice with the gamble task prior the fMRI study.

Sixty of the 160 faces were selected for the fMRI experiment: 20 judged most trustworthy, 20 average and 20 least trustworthy for each participant. Thus, each participant was shown a different set of faces according to their ratings in the behavioural task. So in the context of our trust game these 3 main categories were used to set subjective levels of high, mid and low reward probability (Table 5.1). Given that each main category was further made up of two groups of faces, each assigned to one of two adjacent ratings (e.g. for the high trustworthy category, ratings equal to 10 and 9; for the average category 6 and 5; for the low category 2 and 1), in the follow up fMRI analysis we created 6 reward probability conditions (as well as 3 reward probability conditions reflecting the 3 main categories).

To assess the reliability of the scale used to derive trustworthiness ratings we run a Cronbach's α test on all the scores obtained from the participants. The behavioural session was run on a different day. In addition to the rating task, participants played a similarly modified version of the card game to assess their understanding of the game before the fMRI session (see supplementary Fig.5.1S).

5.2.4 MRI acquisition
Each scanning session started with a localizer scan followed by four functional sessions and with an anatomical scan in between to allow participants to rest.
All sessions were run on a Siemens 3T TimTrio scanner equipped with a 32 channel head coil. Structural scans included T1-weighted images (TR, 2300 ms; TE, 2.96 ms; flip angle, 9°; TI 900 ms; voxel size, 1x1x1 mm; 3D gradient echo pulse sequence T1-MPRAGE, Magnetization Prepared Rapid Gradient Echo). Four functional sessions were run, each of which started off with a localizer scan followed by the gambling paradigm implemented in Presentation (Neurobehavioral Systems) during which T2*-weighted echoplanar images were collected (TR, 1500 ms; TE, 30 ms; flip angle, 70°; 28, 3.5 mm slices interleaved ascending; field of view, 192 mm; voxel size, 3x3x3.5 mm; matrix size 64x64; 440-480 volumes per session).

5.2.5 fMRI preprocessing
Data were preprocessed and analysed using BrainVoyager QX v2.6. Preprocessing included motion correction, slice timing correction, linear drift removal, high-pass filtering, normalisation to Talairach space, and spatial smoothing with a full width at half-maximum

Gaussian kernel of 6 mm. One participant was excluded due excessive head movements. The following fMRI analyses are based on the remaining 20 participants dataset.

5.2.6 fMRI analyses

The statistical analyses of the fMRI data were based on a series of general linear models (GLMs) that can be divided in two parts. For each subject, separate linear models were constructed that included regressors of no interest as well as the regressors described below. Regressors modelled the BOLD response to the specified events using a convolution kernel applied to a boxcar function.

In part 1, to identify the regions of interests (ROIs) correlated to non-social and social uncertainty parameters we created 2 GLMs. GLM1 included parametric modulations of the card game and trust game regressors: early and late reward prediction error. GLM2 included parametric modulations of the card game and trust game regressor risk prediction error.

In part 2, to illustrate how BOLD activity in the identified regions of interest fitted our model we modified the previous GLMs as follows.
GLMs 3 and 4 were created to extract mean sensitivity values for each reward probability level (Tab. 5.1) at card 1 (reward and risk prediction error) and before card 2 (late reward prediction error). GLMs 5 and 6 were created to extract mean sensitivity values and time-course hemodynamic responses for each reward probability level after trustee's face was presented (reward and risk prediction error), and before outcome (late reward prediction error).

GLM1 and GLM2 were set up to run random effects analyses at the group level to locate the mean beta sensitivities to each regressor of interest. For GLM1 and GLM2 the onset regressor at Card 1 (or trustee's face) was divided in two epochs: an early short epoch of one volume and a late long epoch of about 4 volumes depending on the jittered interval until the onset of Card 2 (or outcome coloured square for trust game trials). The first GLM included the modulating parameters early reward prediction error at onset of Card 1 (or trustee's face) and late reward prediction error during the long epoch before Card 2 (or outcome coloured square for trust game trials). GLM2 included the modulating parameter risk prediction error at onset of Card 1 (or trustee's face; both 1 volume long).

Contrasts computed for all parametrically modulated regressors were then tested in separate random effects analyses at the group level. We applied a voxelwise statistical threshold of p=0.05 and corrected for multiple comparisons based on False Discovery Rate (FDR) control for the whole-brain volume.

Figure 5.2 and Table 5.1 give an overview of the mathematical parameters of interest (for further details on calculation of reward and risk parameters see Appendix I).

To illustrate how the BOLD estimates in our ROIs reflected the hypothesised social and non-social uncertainty modulations we created the following GLMs.

In GLM3 the first volume after Card 1 was modelled by ten reward probability regressors. In GLM4 the epoch from volume two to five after Card 1 was modelled by ten reward probability regressors (Table 5.1).

In trust game trials the player's initial choice to trust or not the upcoming trustee generates two sets of conditions (TG-Trust and TG-NoTrust).

In GLM5 the first volume after trustee's face presentation was modelled by two sets of six reward probability regressors (one for TG-Trust and one for TG-NoTrust conditions; Table 5.1). In GLM6 the epoch from volume two to five after trustee's face was modelled by two sets of six reward probability regressors (one for TG-Trust and one for TG-NoTrust conditions).

To test parametric effects in regions that did not pass multiple comparison correction in whole brain analysis and where an a priori region hypothesis was supported by previous findings, we run GLMs 1 and 2 using a small-volume correction of a sphere around the group peak voxels identified from previous studies, and a false-discovery rate (FDR) with a threshold of q(FDR) <0.05. We then used GLMs3-6 to extract the mean beta estimates for each regressor and each subject, averaged the estimates across all subjects and plotted the overall mean estimates against the reward probability values (see Fig. 5.4 and 5.5). Note that these estimates were only used for descriptive plots.

Card game plots for supplementary figures (5.2S, 5.3S, 5.4S) were obtained by averaging the first 3, middle 4 and last 3 reward probability values; whether for trust game plots we averaged the first 2, second 2 and last 2 reward probability values (Table 5.1). In so doing the card game and trust game effects become directly comparable.

Finally to further explore potential sources of interaction between the trustworthiness of the trustee's face and the corresponding level of reward probability in the context of our trust games (TG-Trust and TG-NoTrust), we used mean beta weights extracted from our ROIs in a repeated-measures 2x2 ANOVA comparing high and low trustworthy face conditions (excluding the neutral bin) with high and low reward probability conditions (excluding the mid RePE bin).

5.2.7 Connectivity Analyses: Granger Causality Mapping and Psychophysiological Interaction

Granger causality mapping (GCM) has been used to map functional connectivity in the human brain (Seth et al. 2015; McKay et al. 2012; Schippers et al. 2011; Roebroeck et al. 2005). GCM is used to determine whether the past of time-series X improves the prediction of the values of time-series Y over a given discrete time period (e.g. during task related activity), whether the past of Y improves the prediction of X and the instantaneous correlation between X and Y.

In the context of fMRI analysis GCM is used to determine the directions of influence to and from a reference or seed region by computing three parameters: influence from the seed region to all other voxels in the brain (target voxels), influence from target voxels to the seed region and the instantaneous correlations between seed and target voxels. By subtracting the influence to the seed regions from the influence from the seed regions a differential Granger Causality Map (dGCM) is obtained where positive values represent influence from the seed and negative values represent influence to the seed region (Roebroeck et al. 2005). When used to infer the flow of neural signals in the brain, interpretation of results should be done with caution. In fact GCM can fail to detect intermediate regions in a network. For instance if region A influences B, but for some biological reasons it also influences an intermediate region C which in turn influences B, region C can be missed in the analysis. Nonetheless one important advantage of GCM is that it does not require the a priori specification of a model of directed influence. Researchers have hypothesised that Granger causality might give rise to spurious results in response to differences in hemodynamic response functions between brain areas. Some studies show that spurious findings at the group level of analysis are actually rare, and that GCM is a valid method to determine the dominant direction of information flow (Schippers et al. 2011). Other studies show that even at the group level of analysis the GCM results could be driven by systematic differences in hemodynamic lag between different brain areas (Smith et al. 2012). As we cannot completely exclude this possibility, we will interpret the GCM results as an extension of our parametric analyses and in the context of substantial supporting evidence on the role of the networks studied - e.g. salience network (Menon & Uddin 2010).

We used GCM to examine the flow of neural information to and from bilateral ventral striatum (Fig.5.4), bilateral anterior insula and dACC (Fig. 5.3). We run a GCM for each of these regions of interest and replicated the analysis for both the social and non-social domain throughout the outcome anticipatory window (group fixed effect). This gave ten sets of brain connectivity maps (Fig. 5.6 A-J).

To further support and complement the GCM analysis we also run Psychophysiological Interaction (PPI) analyses using the same regions of interest as our seed regions.

PPI analysis is a particular type of functional connectivity analysis that investigates task-specific changes in the relationship between activity in different brain areas. A PPI analysis identifies which voxels increase their relationship with a seed region of interest (ROI) in a given psychological context (Friston et al. 1997; O'Reilly et al. 2012).

In short, the Brain Voyager (v2.6) PPI plugin used to run the analysis extracted the mean activity of our seed ROIs for each TR. This time course was then z-transformed before to be multiplied TR by TR with the task time course. The result formed a PPI predictor. The task time course was based on the protocol associated with the data. Before to be multiplied by the ROI time course, the task time course was convolved with the haemodynamic response function (McLaren et al. 2012).

For the PPI we divided the anticipatory period in a short epoch (about 1 volume) and a delayed epoch (about 4 volumes) as previously done in the parametric analysis (e.g. GLM1). Therefore for each region of interest the PPI analysis produced two regressors of interest for both the card game (CG1st for the early and CG2nd for the delayed anticipation period; see

Table 5.4) and the trust game (TG1st for the early and TG2nd for the delayed anticipation period; see Table 5.4).

5.3 Results

We first present statistics on task performance. We then describe the results of the whole brain analyses (GLMs 1 and 2) focusing on the outcome anticipation window starting with the onset of the first stimulus (first card or trustee's face) and ending before display of the trial outcome. The results of these analyses are used to define functional regions of interest (ROIs) reflecting coding of reward and risk prediction error. We then carried out ROI based analyses of the properties of the signals encoded in the identified regions (GLMs 3 and 4 for the card game and GLMs 5 and 6 for the trust game), which are used to systematically address the experimental hypotheses. Finally we present results from a functional connectivity analysis using Granger Causality Mapping and Psychophysiological Interaction.

5.3.1 Statistics on behavioural and fMRI task performance

We first assessed the reliability of the scale used to derive perceived trustworthiness ratings in the preliminary behavioural experiment and obtained a Cronbach's $\alpha = 0.82$ indicating high reliability.

In the fMRI task, at time of bet and before the first stimulus is presented, the initial probability of winning in either type of gamble game (card game or trust game) is 0.5. This is reflected in task performance: participants won on 50.37% ($\pm5.04\%$) of all trials. The task also required participants to confirm at the end of each trial that they understood the outcome of the gamble played. This is also reflected in task performance: participants reported the outcome of their bet correctly on 97.85% ($\pm3.78\%$) of all trials suggesting a high level of engagement and accurate representation of the task.

5.3.2 Whole brain parametric analysis of outcome anticipation window

In the non-social domain (card game) our parametric regressor representing RePE correlated with activations in the ventral striatum, putamen and ventral anterior cingulate cortex (ventral ACC) ($p < 0.001$, uncorrected; see Table 5.2 for the list of areas). In addition, our regressor modulated by RiPE covaried with activation in anterior insula, dorsal ACC, dorsolateral prefrontal cortex (dlPFC) and orbitofrontal cortex (OFC) ($p < 0.05$, FDR corrected for the whole brain volume; Table 5.2). Overall, these results reflecting RePE and RiPE signals in the non-social domain are consistent with a large body of literature (Rudorf et al. 2012; Preuschoff et al. 2006; Preuschoff et al. 2008; Schultz et al. 2008) and allow us to directly test the hypothesis of a common currency in the processing of social and non-social uncertainty. In the region of interest analyses we therefore focused on these two fundamental networks: the reward-related network that has been found to correlate with prediction and learning for a wide range of rewarding stimuli (Schultz 2013), and the risk-related network (anterior insula, dorsal ACC and OFC) that more recently has been shown to complement the reward network in the evaluation of outcome anticipation (Preuschoff & Bossaerts 2007; Preuschoff et al. 2008; O'Neill & Schultz 2010; O'Neill & Schultz 2013).

In the social domain (trust game), RePE was found to correlate with activity in a network including regions overlapping with those found in the non-social domain such as the putamen, but also separate regions including the amygdala ($p < 0.001$, uncorrected; see Table 5.3). Analysis of RiPE yielded activation in the midbrain, thalamus, ventral ACC and other regions ($p < 0.001$, uncorrected; see Table 5.3), providing initial evidence of a distinct network processing risk signals in the social and non-social domain of uncertainty.

This result is noteworthy because it also raises the question of whether and how the network encoding RiPE signals in the non-social domain processes uncertainty in the social domain. In the following ROI analyses this experimental question is further examined.

5.3.3 Regions of interest analyses

We identified a distinct network of regions processing degrees of social and non-social uncertainty in the whole brain analysis. Given the growing evidence in favour of BOLD related activity correlated with non-social reward and risk prediction error parameters (Schultz et al. 2008), we next used regions that reflected non-social uncertainty to directly test whether and in what form these regions reflected social uncertainty modulations. We first run this test on a network of regions that significantly reflected coding of risk prediction errors in the non-social domain (Tab. 5.2) including bilateral anterior insula and dorsal ACC. We then run the same test in the ventral striatum, a region that has been found to reflect reward prediction errors (Preuschoff et al. 2006; Pessiglione et al. 2006). Lastly, we report modulations of social uncertainty in amygdala, a region that has been correlated to processing of face trustworthiness (Said et al. 2009) as well as reward anticipation (Holland & Gallagher 2004).

Information about the outcome of the gamble does not vary at the time of bet's decision. Therefore between placing the bet and seeing the first stimulus (either a card or trustee's face) reward and risk prediction remains constant across all trials. The hypothesised uncertainty modulations occur between the first stimulus and the following outcome. Thus the first RePE and RiPE update depends on the first card or trustee's face and varies across trials, allowing to look for a corresponding neural signal. To test this hypothesis we modified the specifications of our general linear models to compare the activation of each reward probability condition within the identified regions of interest.

5.3.4 Early activation in anterior insula and dACC reflects distinct representations of social and non-social prediction errors

Our whole-brain analysis for RiPE replicated previous findings in the non-social domain (Preuschoff et al. 2008; Rudorf et al. 2012) showing that activity in a distributed network including bilateral anterior insula and dorsal ACC, covaried with RiPE ($p < 0.05$, FDR corrected for the whole brain volume; Table 5.2). To directly illustrate how the response profile in these three regions reflected social uncertainty, we plotted mean activation estimates as a function of all possible probability of winning conditions for both card game (CG) and trust game (TG) gambles (Fig. 5.3; see also Fig. 5.2S where card game and trust game effects are more directly comparable).

Similarly to what found in recent studies investigating the non-social domain (Preuschoff et al. 2008; Rudorf et al. 2012), card game plots (CG) show that early activation of these regions following presentation of the first card reflects risk prediction error when modelled as a U-shape function of all reward probability conditions.

Next, in a true out of sample test we directly compared the patterns of activation for trust game trials using the same brain regions. Trust game results (Fig. 5.3) show that early activation following presentation of trustee's face in the same clusters of bilateral anterior insula and dACC is parametrically modulated by the level of uncertainty. This early modulation is positive and linear in the probability of winning and thus cannot reflect risk prediction error but rather a reward prediction error signal (RePE parametric predictor: right anterior insula, $t = 3.80$, $p < 0.0001$; left anterior insula, $t = 2.41$, $p < 0.01$; dACC, $t = 2.87$, $p < 0.004$). We will also discuss whether the modulation observed could reflect a salient prediction error signal - an evaluation of the saliency of the stimulus in the context of the gamble (Metereau & Dreher 2013). On the whole these results suggest that the same distributed network differentially process social and non-social uncertainty.

Importantly, the linear modulation of the fMRI signal following the trustee's face presentation did not simply correlate with trustworthiness per se or low-level visual differences between different types of faces. Crucially, our trust game design allows to test whether modulation of the regions of interest is correlated to the trustworthiness of trustee's face or to the uncertainty the face conveys in the context of the gamble. In fact, the player's initial bet (to decide whether the upcoming partner will share or not at the start of the trust game) generates two sets of conditions where economic uncertainty (as defined by our model) and trustworthiness become orthogonal variables. Indeed, when participants bet that their partner will share at the start of a trust game (Trust condition), they will be more likely to win when seeing a trustworthy face (according to their own pre-rating) as opposed to an untrustworthy face. On the other hand, when participants bet that their partner will not share (No-Trust condition), they will be more likely to win when seeing an untrustworthy face as opposed to a trustworthy face. Therefore if the linear activation in the Trust condition reflected solely changes in face trustworthiness, we should see a negative linear activation in the probability of winning in the No-Trust condition. Our results rule out this interpretation since we found the same positive linear activity in the Trust and No-Trust conditions (orange and violet panels in Fig. 5.3) indicating that the BOLD signal is not correlated with trustworthiness per se but rather with the uncertainty signalled by the trustee's face.

We also tested the effect of the trustworthiness dimension on the reward expectation dimension of the trust games. As we said earlier when betting on Trust one can expect to win when faced with a trustworthy trustee and to lose when faced with one judged untrustworthy. When in turn one plays No-Trust then he should expect to win when faced with an untrustworthy trustee and expect to lose when faced with one judged trustworthy. To further explore this counterintuitive relation between the trustworthiness of the trustee's face on a given trial and the corresponding level of reward probability associated in the No-Trust conditions (as compared to the Trust conditions), we used mean beta weights extracted from our ROIs in a repeated-measures ANOVA that probed the interaction between level of trustworthiness (low or high) and level of reward probability (low or high). The interaction did not reach significance in all three regions (right insula: $F(1,19)=0.33$, $P=0.57$; left insula: $F(1,19)=0.59$, $P=0.45$; dACC: $F(1,19)= 0.39$, $P=0.54$).

5.3.5 Early activation in ventral striatum reflects social and non-social RePE

To compare the beta estimates of RePE for both social and non-social domains, we ran the two GLMs representing the binned reward probability conditions (GLM3 and GLM5 for the card game and trust game respectively; see Methods). We identified two regions of interest (ROI) based on activation peaks reported in previous studies using 3mm spheres around coordinates of ventral striatum (left ventral striatum: $x=-12$; $y=3$; $z=-3$; right ventral striatum: $x=12$; $y=3$; $z=-3$; (Rudorf et al. 2012; Preuschoff et al. 2006). We previously reported activation only of the left ventral striatum in the whole brain analysis for the non-social domain. However the cluster found in our analysis overlaps with the defined ROI sphere (Table 5.2).

Importantly, we found that in both conditions (card game and trust game) the activation of the right ventral striatum covaried with the RePE parametric predictor, increasing linearly in the probability of winning the gamble (CG: $t = 2.68$, $p < 0.007$; TG: $t = 3.05$, $p < 0.002$; see Figure 5.4; see also Fig. 5.3S where card game and trust game effects are more directly comparable). Similarly, in the left ventral striatum, we found that activity encoded RePE for the non-social and social domains and was positively correlated to reward probability (CG: $t = 4.52$, $p < 0.0006$; TG: $t = 2.01$, $p < 0.04$; see Figure 5.4). Overall, these results indicate that at a subcortical level a common neural scale for the processing of social and non-social uncertainty might be employed by the human brain.

We also ran a repeated-measures ANOVA that probed the interaction between level of trustworthiness of the trustee's face (low or high) and level of reward probability (low or high) in the context of our trust game. We found that for both the two clusters of bilateral ventral striatum the interaction did not reach significance (right ventral striatum: $F(1,19)=0.17$, $P=0.68$; left ventral striatum: $F(1,19)=1.8$, $P=0.19$).

5.3.6 Early activation in left amygdala reflects only social RePE

So far we have shown that, across the social and non-social domains of uncertainty, same regions similarly (ventral striatum) or differentially (anterior insula and dACC) encode reward and risk prediction errors respectively. One region, however, seems to be solely processing RePE in the social domain. Indeed the whole brain analysis revealed activity in the left amygdala correlating with the social RePE parametric predictor (Table 2) whereas it did not appear in the non-social condition. To further explore the response profile of the amygdala to social RePE, we extracted bilaterally mean beta values from a larger region of 5 mm sphere around the mean peak from whole brain analysis (left amygdala: $x=-20$; $y=-7$; $z=-15$). We found that only activations in left amygdala correlated with the early RePE predictor as well as with the late RePE (early predictor: $t = 2.38$, $p < 0.01$; late predictor: $t = 3.35$, $p < 0.0008$). Figure 5.5 shows mean beta values reflecting a positive linear activation in reward probability (top plots show early and bottom plots late RePE; see also Fig. 5.4S where card game and trust game effects are more directly comparable). Importantly, this result is consistent with evidence in the literature suggesting a role of amygdala in processing face trustworthiness (Said et al. 2009; Todorov et al. 2013) as well as reward anticipation (Holland & Gallagher 2004). We also ran a repeated-measures ANOVA that probed the interaction between level of trustworthiness of the trustee's face (low or high) and level of reward probability (low or high) in the context of our trust game. We found that the interaction between level of trustworthiness of trustee's face and level of reward probability was not significant ($F(1,19)=3.3$, $P=0.08$).

5.3.7 Granger Causality Mapping and Psychophysiological Interaction analyses reveal a distinct functional connectivity between social and non-social domain

Taken together, our results expose equivalences and differences between social and non-social reward and risk processing in the human brain. Specifically, while non-social and social RePE seems to be encoded in a similar fashion in dopaminergic subcortical areas, the network involved in processing non-social RiPE fundamentally differs in its response to modulations of social uncertainty. We further investigated the connectivity between the key regions involved in both domains to further clarify the potential role of each area in orchestrating probabilistic stimulus-reward associations. We therefore ran functional connectivity analyses using Granger Causality Mapping (GCM), (Seth et al. 2015; Roebroeck et al. 2005), and Psychophysiological Interaction (PPI), (O'Reilly et al. 2012; Friston et al. 1997), on the ventral striatum, dACC and bilateral anterior insula.

In the GCM and PPI analyses we used the clusters illustrated in figure 5.3 and 5.4 as our reference regions for both social and non-social domains. In the GCM analysis this produced brain maps showing source and target activations illustrating functional connectivity throughout the outcome anticipation window. Target activations represent regions consistently activated in time after the seed region and thus are hypothesised to be causally influenced by the seed region (our reference regions). Source activations represent regions whose activation consistently preceded in time that of the seed region and thus are hypothesised to have a causal influence on the neural activation of the seed region. For each region of interest the PPI analysis produced two regressors of interest for both the card game (CG1st for the early and CG2nd for the delayed anticipation period; see Table 5.4) and the trust game (TG1st for the early and TG2nd for the delayed anticipation period; see Table 5.4).

The connectivity analyses further supported the hypothesis that the activity found in bilateral anterior insula and dACC (Fig. 5.3) during the outcome anticipation window is functionally related (Fig. 5.6). This also shed light on the underlying dynamics that might be responsible for the differential response profile found in cortical regions for social and non-social types of uncertainty (Fig. 5.7).

More in detail in the GCM analysis we found that in the non-social domain right anterior insula receives neural information from the left anterior insula (Fig. 5.6-A). This is further confirmed when left anterior insula is set as reference region (Fig. 5.6-B). Right and left anterior insula send information to a region partially overlapping with the dACC cluster. In turn dACC is influenced by right anterior insula, while it influences a cluster of the cuneus in visual areas (Fig. 5.6-C). Only right anterior insula receives neural input from a region of the putamen (Fig. 5.6-A). Importantly, all three seed regions (bilateral anterior insula and dACC) receive from ventromedial prefrontal cortex (vmPFC) and bilateral orbitofrontal cortex (OFC). Lastly, the right ventral striatum influences right amygdala (Fig. 5.6-D), while the left ventral striatum influences the left OFC (Fig. 5.6-E). The PPI analysis provided further correlational support to the picture depicted by the GCM analysis in the non-social domain (Table 5.4). In addition to the regions found using GCM, the PPI revealed greater connectivity of the left anterior insula and left ventral striatum clusters with the dlPFC (t=3.91, P<0.003, early anticipation period; t=4.05, P<0.002, delayed anticipation period), and of the right ventral striatum with the thalamus (t=3.86, P<0.004, delayed anticipation period).

In the social domain right anterior insula sends neural information to left anterior insula (Fig. 5.6-F). This is further confirmed when left anterior insula is set as reference region (Fig. 5.6-G). In turn the dACC influences both right and left anterior insula (Fig. 5.6-H). Only left anterior insula sends neural input to a region of the putamen (Fig. 5.6-G). Interestingly, right anterior insula and dACC both influence the OFC. Lastly, the right ventral striatum influences the contralateral left ventral striatum, left anterior insula and vmPFC, and is influenced by a region of the midbrain, right anterior insula, vmPFC, OFC and dACC (Fig. 5.6-I). The left ventral striatum influences the contralateral right ventral striatum, anterior insula and vmPFC, and is influenced by midbrain, right vmPFC, OFC and dACC (Fig. 5.6-J). Also in the social domain the PPI analysis besides indicating connectivity with most regions found in GCM provides some further insight (Table 5.4). Both the dACC and left ventral striatum clusters show correlational connectivity with the thalamus (dACC: t=-6.99, P<0.05 FDR corrected, delayed anticipation period; left ventral striatum: t=-5.43, P<0.002, delayed anticipation period). Importantly PPI showed evidence of functional connectivity between the left anterior insula cluster and bilateral amygdala (left amygdala: t=-4.70, P<0.05 FDR corrected, delayed anticipation period; right amygdala: t=-3.91, P<0.05 FDR corrected, delayed anticipation period).

Figure 5.7 shows a schematic model of the described flow of neural information between reference regions and target and source regions (GCM), and put it in relation with the specific neural modulation profile found for social and non-social uncertainty (Fig. 5.3 and 5.4). Critically the model shows that functional connectivity between cortical and subcortical regions differs between the social and non-social domains.

5.4 Discussion

We directly compared activation patterns due to reward anticipation in a social game with those due to anticipation of non-social financial rewards. We focused on how social and non-social experimental manipulations affected the neural coding of expected reward and risk while keeping value constant.

We used a trust betting game to vary uncertainty along a social dimension (trustworthiness). Concurrently we used a card game (Preuschoff et al. 2006) to vary uncertainty along a non-social dimension (pure risk). The social trust game was designed to replicate and maintain the same structure of the non-social card game.

To test our first hypothesis we first run whole brain parametric analyses to locate regions distinctively responding to either social or non-social modulations of uncertainty (Table 5.2 and 5.3). Results showed that largely similar subcortical regions would represent RePE in the social and non-social domain, while at the cortical level RePE and RiPE are represented differentially.

We then reasoned that one way to test our second hypothesis would be to identify regions of interest parametrically modulated by one type of gamble (non-social card game) and then use those same regions to test parametric modulations on the other type of gamble (social trust game). Given the growing evidence supporting the idea that a specific network of regions encodes RePEs and RiPEs in the non-social domain, a direct comparison of social and non-social response profiles within these regions could further reveal whether the response profile to different degrees of uncertainty was similar as hypothesised or not. We then replicated previous findings (Preuschoff et al. 2006; Preuschoff et al. 2008; Rudorf et al. 2012) and located a network of regions that reflected coding of RePE and RiPE in the non-social domain and used those regions of interest to see whether they reflected coding of uncertainty in the social domain. In line with our hypothesis we found that activity in bilateral ventral striatum correlated with both social and non-social RePE (Fig. 5.4), whereas activity in amygdala reflected only social RePE (Fig. 5.5). Interestingly, in contrast with our initial hypothesis we found that a network of regions including bilateral anterior insula and dorsal anterior cingulate cortex (dACC) coding for RiPE in the non-social domain, reflected modulation of social uncertainty with a different response profile (RePE-like; Fig. 5.3).

5.4.1 Anterior insula and the RePE hypothesis

The insular cortex has been traditionally implicated in the integration of bodily states and affective values (Craig 2009). More recently anterior insula activity has been found to correlate with uncertainty (Huettel et al. 2006), risk prediction error (Preuschoff et al. 2008) and subjective risk preferences when people play non-social pure risk gambles (Rudorf et al. 2012). This evidence further supports the observation that damage to this structure leads to anomalous behaviour in the context of uncertainty (Bechara & Damasio 2005). On the whole this view dismiss the idea that anterior insula should be seen as a mere relay station of bodily states but rather a centre that integrates uncertainty with bodily, affective and sensory information in a quantitative manner (Preuschoff et al. 2008; Singer et al. 2009).

Our data show that coding of prediction errors in anterior insula extends to the domain of social uncertainty when this is represented by parametric modulations of face trustworthiness (Fig. 5.3). Crucially, this neural representation differs when the discrepancy in the prediction of reward or risk (RePE and RiPE) is presented in social or non-social form. We found that in the non-social domain bilateral anterior insula reflects RiPE as a U-shaped function of reward probability (Fig. 5.3). The same clusters in anterior insula represent social discrepancies in the prediction of outcome as a linear function of reward probability. We also explored whether betting on No-Trust had an effect on the anticipation of reward (compared to betting on Trust) and found no interactions.

This result suggests that BOLD activity in these regions reflects coding of RePE when different degrees of social uncertainty signal outcome anticipation. Several studies have identified RePE model correlations in the anterior insula (Seymour et al. 2004; Voon et al. 2010; Pessiglione et al. 2006). We found a similar parametric modulation of social uncertainty in other regions of the brain traditionally associated with coding of RePE such as ventral striatum (Fig. 5.4; Table 5.2). However it is important to note that in the context of non-social decision-making it has been debated whether activity in anterior insula could reflect processing of RePE. One study (Rutledge et al. 2010) used a previously developed axiomatic approach (Caplin & Dean 2007; Caplin & Dean 2008) to perform an empirical test on brain activations (fMRI) in areas strongly innervated with dopaminergic terminations. They found that insula activation violated two of the three axioms of reward prediction error theory. Their conclusion was that the activity in insula as measured by BOLD could not serve as a reward prediction error encoder. While these results represent compelling evidence in the non-social domain, they cannot be directly extended to social uncertainty.

5.4.2 Anterior insula, dACC and the salience prediction error hypothesis

In addition we observed a similar social uncertainty modulation in dACC (Fig. 5.3). This structure has been implicated in reward-based decision-making, learning, error detection and most recently processing of subjective risk preferences and dynamic risk taking (Bush et al. 2002; Leiby 2009; Kolling et al. 2014; Rudorf et al. 2012). Evidence from brain imaging research encompassing several task domains shows that ACC and anterior insula activity reflects the degree of subjective salience (Craig 2009). Furthermore anterior insula and ACC have been found to share a critical feature at the neuronal level in the human brain. Both structures contain a proportion of specialised brain cells known as von Economo neurons (Allman et al. 2010). These neurons, also called spindle neurons for their characteristic shape, possess large axons that can facilitate rapid communication and it is therefore speculated that they constitute the neuronal basis of fast control signals generated in the salience network connecting anterior insula and regions of the ACC (Menon & Uddin 2010; Seth 2013).

Activity in both structures, ACC and anterior insula, has been recently found to reflect salient prediction errors. One study used a model-based fMRI approach combined with a Pavlovian conditioning procedure to test regions of the brain responding similarly to prediction errors conditioned by stimuli carrying opposite valence but same salience (Metereau & Dreher 2013). This study revealed that both favourable and aversive conditioned stimuli (e.g. rewards and punishments) reflected a similar salient predictor error in bilateral anterior insula and ACC.

We found a distinct neural response to modulation of social uncertainty in a group of areas including anterior insula and dACC, key regions of the salience network (Menon & Uddin 2010). This network though anchored in anterior insula and dACC is connected extensively to the limbic structures involved in reward processing and is thought to identify the most relevant among internal and external stimuli in order to guide behaviour (Seeley et al. 2007).

Nonetheless it is important to note that the modulation observed for social and non-social uncertainty (Fig. 5.2 and 5.3) could not represent a salient prediction error. In fact the paradigm employed has been shown to minimise the effect of learning and salience

(Preuschoff et al. 2006). Although the U-shape activation observed in the non-social domain (Fig. 5.2) could suggest a salient prediction error interpretation, a closer look reveals otherwise. While it is true that high probability of wins or losses is a salient event, a similar argument can be put forward for when uncertainty (prediction risk) is highest at p=0.5, thus discarding the salient prediction error interpretation.

Similarly in the social domain one could observe that regardless of the stimulus being aversive (untrustworthy trustee) or favourable (trustworthy trustee) lower expected reward is always reflected in a lower BOLD response and higher expected reward is always reflected in a higher BOLD response (Fig. 5.3). This would imply though that in the context of social decision making and trust a lower expected reward is less salient than a higher expected reward.

Finally, although salient prediction error effects have been reported in these regions (Metereau & Dreher 2013), our study was not specifically designed to disentangle the effect of signed as opposed to unsigned or salient prediction errors in the neural coding of uncertainty.

5.4.3 Functional connectivity of cortical and subcortical ROIs

We also asked what are the partner regions responsible for the observed differential response to non-social pure risk and social uncertainty gambles. One hypothesis to put to test involves the role of dorsolateral prefrontal cortex (dlPFC) within the central-executive network and its interaction with the salience network (Menon & Uddin 2010). Further investigation is therefore needed to assess the role of interacting networks involved in processing different forms of uncertainty. Transcranial Magnetic Stimulation (TMS) could further reveal the causal role of dlPFC in the neural coding of social uncertainty in anterior insula and dACC.

Another related hypothesis is that different nodes of the salience network (different subregions of the anterior insula and ACC) could facilitate the detection of stimuli representing different forms of uncertainty. In fact, what makes the salience network crucial among the multiple salience filters along the ascending pathways bringing sensory stimuli to the cortical stations is its cognitive control (Menon & Uddin 2010). In this sense, different nodes of the network could trigger distinct cascades of cognitive control signals that determine how one or the other type of uncertainty will be subsequently processed.

To address some of the issues laid out, we used Granger Causality Mapping (GCM) and Psychophysiological Interaction (PPI) to test functional connectivity in key regions of interest. These connectivity analyses further supported the hypothesis that the activation found in bilateral anterior insula and dACC (Fig. 5.3) is functionally related in both social and non-social domains (Fig. 5.6; Table 5.4). Furthermore, an overall view of functional connectivity provided a better understanding of the neural dynamics underlying the differential response profile found in cortical regions for social and non-social types of uncertainty. To summarise these analyses we produced a model of functional connectivity between cortical and subcortical regions, illustrating how this differs between the social and non-social domains (Fig. 5.7). In the non-social domain cortical regions seem to influence and being influenced by subcortical regions to a much lesser extent compared to the social domain. This observation is not surprising when related to the different response profiles found for social and non-social uncertainty (Fig. 5.3 and 5.4). In fact, in the social domain the response profile for outcome anticipation (RePE) is the same for subcortical and cortical regions. This is reflected in a wider functional connectivity between these two groups of regions. On the contrary, in the non-social domain the response profile for outcome anticipation is distinct for subcortical (RePE) and cortical regions (RiPE). This is also reflected in our functional connectivity as it suggests a lower level of influence between subcortical and cortical regions.

It is interesting to note that the PPI analysis suggested a role of the thalamus in both the social and non-social domain that was not picked up by the GCM analysis. In particular in the social domain both the dACC and left ventral striatum clusters are negatively correlated with a region of the thalamus (Table 5.4). This is intriguing when considering that in the GCM analysis of the social domain the dACC acts as a source region to the left ventral striatum when this is set as seed region, and leads to hypothesise a functional role of the thalamus as a mid-way station connecting the two regions. Furthermore, though we did not find significant functional connectivity in the GCM with amygdala during outcome anticipation, the PPI analysis revealed connectivity between the left anterior insula cluster and bilateral amygdala (Table 5.4). This is interesting in light of the results from the parametric analysis revealing that only left amygdala was specifically involved in processing social prediction errors (Fig. 5.5).

Finally, it is important to consider that interpretation of GCM results should be made with caution. We previously laid out some of the problems that the technique might face when used to interpret brain activity. Here we should also note that the most reliable influences in GCM are those that vary with experimental condition (Roebroeck et al. 2005). This is because potential confounds in structural hemodynamic variations should not vary with changes in task related conditions. For instance the influence from region A to B found in a GCM in principle could be due to differences in hemodynamic. A and B could generally covary in their activity and microvascular differences could be the cause for a larger hemodynamic response delay in B, delaying its fluctuations in the BOLD signal with respect to A. However this difference can be assigned to interactions between neuronal populations if it can be shown to be modulated by experimental conditions. Therefore when functional connectivity influences are modulated by experimental conditions (e.g. social vs non-social domain of uncertainty), this type of confound should be discarded as an underlying reason for the influence.

5.4.4 Right and left anterior insula lateralisation

Interestingly, the cluster in right anterior insula was bigger than the one in left anterior insula. There is some evidence of lateralisation effects in the literature on anterior insula [see (Duerden et al. 2013) for a meta-analysis of 143 fMRI studies]. In some studies sensory information about the body's state (Craig 2009), valence (Späti et al. 2014) or risk related activity (Pessiglione et al. 2006; Paulus & Stein 2006) has been reported with some degree of lateralisation in right anterior insula. In our connectivity analysis we noted that in the non-social domain the right anterior insula receives neural inputs from the left. One possible explanation for the stronger activation observed is that the BOLD signal is mainly driven by the biological processes underlying postsynaptic activity (Lauritzen 2005). Hence the stronger BOLD recorded in the right anterior insula that receives the synaptic inputs from the left.

5.4.5 Amygdala selective response to degrees of social uncertainty

The amygdala is part of a circuit which includes the dopamine system (Baxter & Murray 2002). Traditionally the amygdala has been viewed as the fear centre of the brain (LeDoux

2007; Adolphs et al. 1995). More recently it has been associated with goal-directed learning and reward anticipation (Baxter & Murray 2002; Holland & Gallagher 2004). However, the two views can be reconciled. Fear may be the emotional expression of estimation uncertainty, just like arousal relates to positive reward prediction errors and activation of the dopamine system (Bossaerts 2009). For instance when faced with ambiguous situations fear may act as a dual signal, relaying both a message not to risk and to find out more (Hsu et al. 2005).

Amygdala is rarely found activated in non-social pure risk tasks (like our card game) where outcome probabilities are known (Bossaerts 2010). Rather it emerges as a crucial brain region in situations of ambiguity where outcome probabilities are not known (Hsu et al. 2005). This is also the case in our trust game where outcome probabilities are not explicit. In fact, we found that left but not right amygdala activity is positively correlated with RePE during anticipation of outcome only in the social domain of uncertainty (Fig. 5.5). This finding is interesting as other evidence suggests that the left amygdala in particular plays a role in the brain's reward system (Whalen & Phelps 2009). Lateralisation in amygdala response to socially relevant stimuli has been documented recently in a meta-analysis study (Mende-Siedlecki et al. 2012). The analysis of the contrasts showing stronger neural responses to negative (i.e. attractive or trustworthy) faces than to positive (i.e. unattractive or untrustworthy) faces revealed consistent activation only in the right amygdala. This result suggests that the reason we did not see an equivalent response in right amygdala might be related to this region being specialised in detecting positive or negative visual fixtures of the face per se, rather than the reward uncertainty carried by them.

Interestingly, some studies showed amygdala nonlinear responses to valence/trustworthiness with stronger responses to positive-looking and negative-looking faces than faces in the middle of the continuum (Todorov & Oosterhof 2011; Said et al. 2009). In particular, Said and collaborators (2009) found that the BOLD response was higher towards both extremes of the trustworthiness scale, and lower for faces deemed as average trustworthy. This study did not imply decision-making or reward expectation but only passive viewing of human faces. Nonetheless given the role that amygdala plays in reward processing one can hypothesise that such a non-linear response could reflect processing of social uncertainty. That is, lower activation found in amygdala for average trustworthy faces could represent higher perceived uncertainty, whereas higher activation observed towards the extremes of the trustworthiness dimension could represent lower perceived uncertainty. Furthermore as noted by the authors in their discussion, a nonlinear response profile is inconsistent with functional descriptions of the amygdala as a detector of fear or negative stimuli. Rather it is consistent with the idea that the amygdala detects salience. Our data might help interpret further this salience hypothesis. In our trust game changes in expectation of reward are reflected in changes in amygdala's activation such that an untrustworthy face can drive a very similar activation as a very trustworthy face. And this is what Said and collaborators (2009) seem to have measured in their experiment. Being our fMRI task explicitly designed to modulate reward uncertainty using face trustworthiness we were able to measure the full spectrum of possible activations. In Said et al. (2009) uncertainty was not manipulated (subjects were passively watching the faces being presented), and it seems plausible that the activation they measured is the result of a non-specific salience detection activity in amygdala - faces least and most trustworthy being generally more salient than average trustworthy faces resulted in higher amygdala activation. Thus our results suggest that a decision-making paradigm might be effectively employed in the study of face trustworthiness in general. As this social dimension is highly correlated with uncertainty, one can disentangle the two only by using an appropriate orthogonal design. To do so a decision-making task could prove more effective than passive viewing of stimuli to separate the effect of reward uncertainty from that of trustworthiness per se in face perception.

5.4.6 Conclusion

Although processing of social and non-social forms of uncertainty seems to rely on largely similar subcortical networks, our data suggests that in some of the key cortical regions processing reward uncertainty the response profile differs between the two domains.

On the one hand activity in subcortical regions such as the ventral striatum during outcome anticipation reflect RePE in both social and non-social domains. In contrast activity in cortical regions such as anterior insula and dACC during outcome anticipation does not reflect a similar neural profile in both domains. In fact we found that activity in these regions correlate with RiPE in the non-social domain and with RePE in the social domain.

Overall these results suggest that identical neural populations can compute discrepancies in the prediction of outcomes using similar or different computations for social and non-social uncertainty. Finally, the study offers a view into how fundamentally different types of uncertainty can be directly compared, as well as generating new open questions for further investigation.

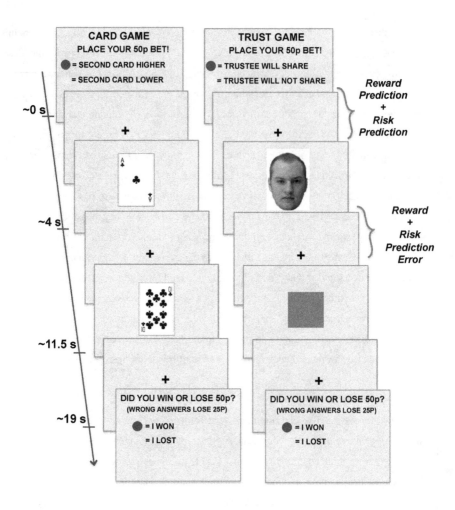

Figure 5.1. Gambling paradigm.

Participants played card game (CG) and trust game (TG) trials presented in random order. In card game trials they first bet on the second card presented being higher or lower than the first one. In trust game trials they bet on whether the trustee associated to that game was going to return a share or not. The timeline of the two types of gamble is identical. After placing their bet participants watch the first card or trustee's face followed 7.5s later by a second card or a coloured square (green=trustee shared; red=trustee kept). Finally participants were asked to confirm if they won or lost on that gamble. With display of the first card or trustee's face the initial constant reward and risk prediction is only partially resolved and a reward and risk prediction error occurs.

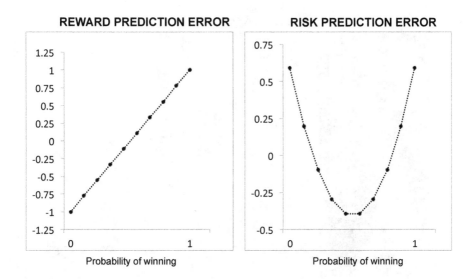

Figure 5.2. Decision parameters functions.

Plots illustrate reward prediction error and risk prediction error as a function of the probability of winning after display of Card 1. Before Card 1 (or trustee's face) is revealed reward and risk prediction are constant. After Card 1 is revealed the error becomes a function of the probability of winning. Reward prediction error is linear and risk prediction error is quadratic (U-shaped) in the probability of winning (more details can be found in Appendix I).

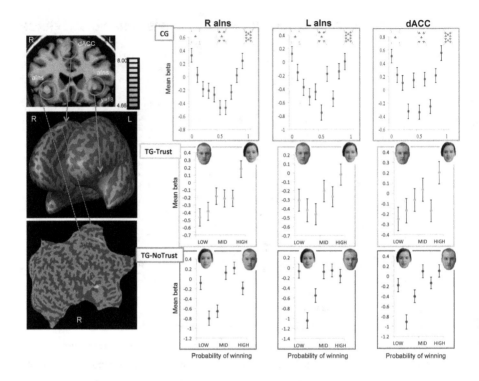

Figure 5.3. Neural differentiation of social and non-social uncertainty during outcome anticipation.

Figures (from top left: coronal view, bilateral inflated cortex, flattened right cortical sheet) show statistical parametric maps of the random effect analysis colour coded for the t-values (p<0.05, FDR corrected for the whole brain volume, df=19). Plots (first row) show that neural activation in bilateral anterior insula (aIns) and dorsal anterior cingulate cortex (dACC) to card game trials (CG) correlates positively with risk prediction error after first card. This first prediction error update is represented as a U-shaped function of 10 reward probability conditions (x-axis represents probability of winning; see also Methods). Activation in the same regions to both trust game subgroups of trials (TG-Trust and TG-NoTrust) correlates positively with a linear function of reward probability conditions as of display of trustee face (x-axis, from left to right, represents ascending reward probability conditions). Error bars=SE.

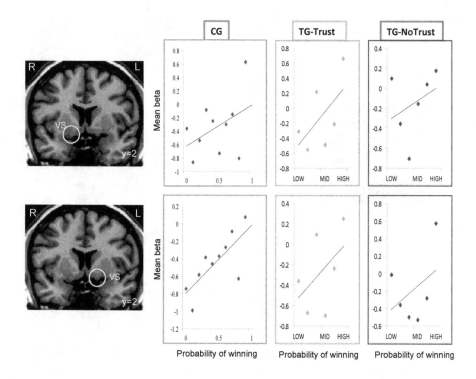

Figure 5.4. Neural differentiation of social and non-social uncertainty in ventral striatum reflects RePE.

Figures (coronal view) show ROIs consisting of 3mm spheres around coordinates of ventral striatum (VS; left ventral striatum: x=-12; y=3; z=-3; right ventral striatum: x=12; y=3; z=-3). Plots show that neural activation to card game trials (CG) correlates positively with reward prediction error (RePE) after first card in bilateral ventral striatum. This first prediction error update is represented as a linear function of 10 reward probability conditions (x-axis represents probability of winning; see also Methods). Similarly activation in the same regions to both trust game subgroups of trials (TG-Trust and TG-NoTrust) correlates positively with a linear function of reward probability conditions as of display of trustee face (x-axis, from left to right, represents ascending reward probability conditions).

97

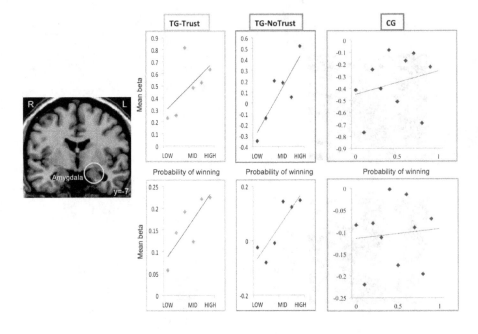

Figure 5.5. Neural differentiation of social uncertainty in left amygdala reflects RePE.

Figure (coronal view) shows ROI consisting of 5mm spheres around coordinates of left amygdala (centre coordinates: x=-20; y=-7; z=-15). Plots show that early (top raw) and late (bottom raw) neural activation in left amygdala to both trust game subgroups of trials (TG-Trust and TG-NoTrust) correlates positively with a linear function of reward probability conditions as of display of trustee face (x-axis, from left to right, represents ascending reward probability conditions).

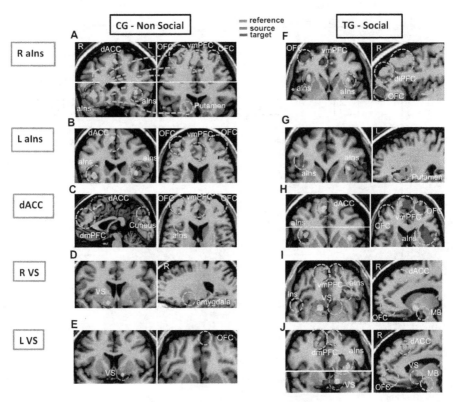

Figure 5.6. Functional connectivity analysis during outcome anticipation for social and non-social uncertainty conditions.

Connections between regions are shown on axial, coronal and sagittal slices. These show the overlaps between the regions of interest and the map returned by the GCM analysis for five reference regions (yellow regions within red circles): bilateral anterior insula (aIns), dorsal anterior cingulate cortex (dACC) and bilateral ventral striatum. Blue and green maps (target and source regions) indicate the direction of influence: blue indicates that activity in the reference region influences activity in the target region; green indicates that activity in the source region influences activity in the reference region. Overall maps show connectivity between our reference regions, indicating that these clusters defined functionally are part of a network. Maps also show how activity in reference regions influences and is influenced by a wider network including cortical and subcortical clusters.

Regions abbreviations: aIns (anterior insula); dACC (dorsal anterior cingulate cortex); OFC (orbitofrontal cortex); vmPFC (ventromedial prefrontal cortex); dmPFC (dorsomedial prefrontal cortex); dlPFC (dorsolateral prefrontal cortex); VS (ventral striatum); MB (midbrain).

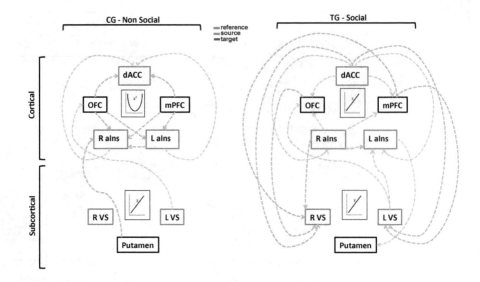

Figure 5.7. Model of functional connectivity and response profile for social and non-social uncertainty derived from GCM.

Blue and green arrows indicate the direction of influence between reference regions (in red boxes) and source and target regions. In particular, blue always indicates influence from a reference region (red box) to a target region. Green always indicates influence from a source region to a reference region (red box).

In both social and non-social domain, regions are grouped in cortical and subcortical. Each group is also paired with a response profile type (either linear or quadratic) as found in our analysis of outcome anticipation (Fig. 5.3 and 5.4).

Overall the model shows differences in connectivity between the social and non-social domain. Not only functional connectivity differs in cortical regions but most importantly between these and the subcortical regions, proving further evidence to interpret the different response profile found for social and non-social uncertainty.

Regions abbreviations: aIns (anterior insula); dACC (dorsal anterior cingulate cortex); OFC (orbitofrontal cortex); mPFC (medial prefrontal cortex); VS (ventral striatum).

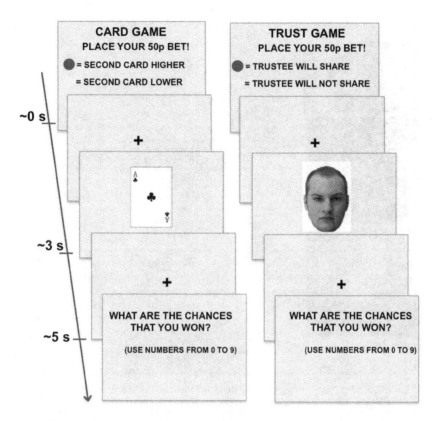

Figure 5.1S. Behavioural study paradigm.

Trust game. On each trial before seeing the trustee's face participants first placed a bet choosing one of two options: "trustee will share" or "trustee will not share", then trustee's face was shown. Participants won if they guessed whether the trustee decided to share or not. Once the bet was placed, participants saw the trustee's face, followed 1s later by a fixation cross. Then a message appeared asking to indicate, using a 0-9 scale, the likelihood of winning the game.

Card game. On each trial, two cards were drawn (without replacement within each trial) from a deck of ten, numbered 1 through 10. Before seeing either card, participants first place a bet on one of two options: "second card higher" or "second card lower", then the first card was shown. Once the bet was placed, participants saw card 1, followed 1s later by a fixation cross. Then a message appeared asking to indicate using a 0-9 scale, the likelihood of winning the game.

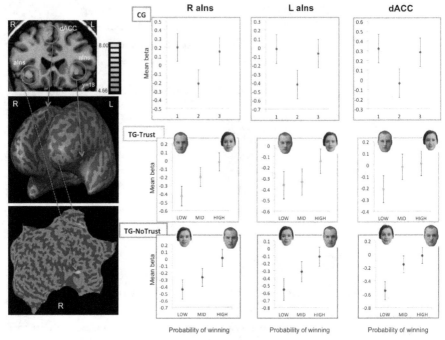

Figure 5.2S. Neural differentiation of social and non-social uncertainty during outcome anticipation. Figures (from top left: coronal view, bilateral inflated cortex, flattened right cortical sheet) show statistical parametric maps of the random effect analysis colour coded for the t-values (p<0.05, FDR corrected for the whole brain volume, df=19). Plots (first row) show that neural activation in bilateral anterior insula (aIns) and dorsal anterior cingulate cortex (dACC) to card game trials (CG) correlates positively with risk prediction error after first card. This first prediction error update is represented as a U-shaped function of the 3 averaged reward probability levels (x-axis, from left to right, represents ascending reward probability conditions; see also Methods). Activation in the same regions to both trust game subgroups of trials (TG-Trust and TG-NoTrust) correlates positively with a linear function of reward probability conditions as of display of trustee face (x-axis, from left to right, represents ascending reward probability conditions). Error bars=SE.

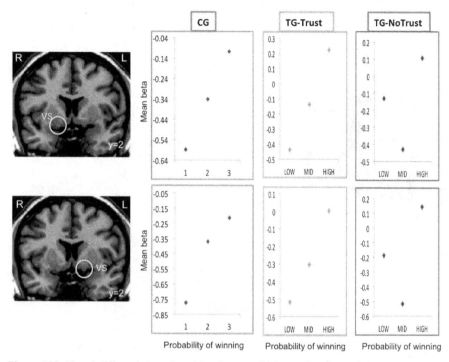

Figure 5.3S. Neural differentiation of social and non-social uncertainty in ventral striatum reflects RePE.

Figures (coronal view) show ROIs consisting of 3mm spheres around coordinates of ventral striatum (VS; left ventral striatum: x=-12; y=3; z=-3; right ventral striatum: x=12; y=3; z=-3). Plots show that neural activation to card game trials (CG) correlates positively with reward prediction error (RePE) after first card in bilateral ventral striatum. This first prediction error update is represented as a linear function of the 3 averaged reward probability levels (x-axis, from left to right, represents ascending reward probability conditions; see also Methods). Similarly activation in the same regions to both trust game subgroups of trials (TG-Trust and TG-NoTrust) correlates positively with a linear function of reward probability conditions as of display of trustee face (x-axis, from left to right, represents ascending reward probability conditions).

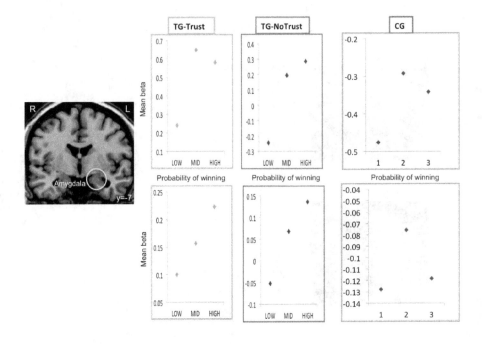

Figure 5.4S. Neural differentiation of social uncertainty in left amygdala reflects RePE.

Figure (coronal view) shows ROI consisting of 5mm spheres around coordinates of left amygdala (centre coordinates: x=-20; y=-7; z=-15). Plots show that early and late neural activation in left amygdala to both trust game subgroups of trials (TG-Trust and TG-NoTrust) correlates positively with a linear function of reward probability conditions as of display of trustee face (x-axis, from left to right, represents ascending reward probability conditions).

Table 5.1. Card game and trust game decision parameters values.

Reward Probability at Card 1 (p)	RePE	RiPE
0*	-1	0.59
0.11*	-0.78	0.20
0.22	-0.56	-0.10
0.33	-0.33	-0.30
0.44**	-0.11	-0.40
0.56**	0.11	-0.40
0.67	0.33	-0.30
0.78	0.56	-0.10
0.89***	0.78	0.20
1***	1	0.59

The table shows all decision parameter values for reward prediction error (RePE), and risk prediction error (RiPE) corresponding to each initial reward probability condition at Card 1 (mathematical details can be found in Appendix I).

*Corresponding values for low reward probability in trust game trials.

**Corresponding values for mid reward probability in trust game trials.

***Corresponding values for high reward probability in trust game trials.

Table 5.2. Regions positively correlated with non-social pure risk parameters (card game).

Region	Laterality	Talairach coordinates			Cluster size	Max stat t
		x	y	z		
Reward prediction error						
Ventral striatum	L	-15	1	-8	133	5.38
Putamen	R	17	15	11	334	4.92
Anterior cingulate cortex	R	116	110	106	242	4.91
Risk prediction error						
Anterior insula	R	32	21	0	732	7.42*
	L	-32	19	0	287	5.92*
Dorsal ACC	R	4	22	43	819	6.89*
	L	-5	11	50	171	5.60*
Inferior frontal gyrus/OFC	R	46	25	-2	42	4.85*
Middle frontal gyrus/dlPFC	R	38	24	27	71	5.45*

Summary of random-effect analyses (for more details see Methods).
* $p < 0.05$ (activation survives correction for multiple comparisons, FDR corrected for the whole brain volume). Otherwise $p < 0.001$, uncorrected.

Table 5.3. Regions positively correlated with social uncertainty parameters (trust game).

Region	Laterality	Talairach coordinates			Cluster size	Max stat t
		x	y	z		
Reward prediction error						
Ventral striatum*	R	8	4	-8	71	4.20
Putamen	R	26	9	7	99	3.49
Caudate head*	R	5	22	1	120	5.37
	L	-8	21	1	28	4.05
Amygdala*	L	-17	-12	-12	116	5.19
Anterior insula	R	41	11	12	137	3.49
Inferior frontal gyrus/OFC	R	48	34	0	323	3.70
OFC (BA 10)*	L	-10	38	-4	378	4.31
Superior frontal gyrus/dlPFC*	L	-18	37	48	171	4.47
Risk prediction error						
Midbrain	R	10	-23	-4	21	3.79
Thalamus	L	-11	-25	0	101	4.34
Parahippocampal gyrus	R	33	-46	0	331	6.39
Anterior cingulate cortex	L	-13	28	15	114	4.88
Fusiform gyrus	R	33	-75	-12	201	5.32

Summary of random-effect analyses ($p < 0.001$, uncorrected).
*Regions correlated to the late RePE parametric predictor (for more details see Methods).

Table 5.4. Results from PPI analysis.

PPI Seed ROI - Regressor - Region	Laterality	Talairach coordinates			Cluster size	Max stat t
		x	y	z		
Left Anterior Insula						
CG1st						
Anterior Insula	R	34	21	2	704	-4.91
Dorsal ACC	R	5	21	53	1961	-5.47
dlPFC (BA9)	L	-18	36	20	50	3.91
OFC (BA10)	R	24	56	12	180	-4.11
CG2nd						
Dorsal ACC	R	8	29	45	41	3.71
Anterior Insula	R	25	19	12	26	3.75
TG1st						
Anterior Insula	R	35	23	5	1239	-5.93
vmPFC	R	12	42	0	118	5.41
TG2nd						
Amygdala*	L	-29	-5	-17	76	-4.70
	R	30	-11	-16	95	-3.91
Insula*	R	47	-6	13	1106	-5.04
Putamen*	R	20	4	-1	45	-3.89
Right Anterior Insula						
CG1st						
Dorsal ACC	L	-4	12	47	1570	-4.97
Ventral ACC	L	-4	32	6	92	4.92
CG2nd						
dlPFC (BA46)	L	-47	32	6	378	-6.06
TG1st						
Anterior Insula	L	-41	18	1	691	-5.22
TG2nd						
mPFC*	R	7	48	21	266	-6.28
OFC*	L	-14	59	21	140	-5.17
Right dACC						
CG1st						
Putamen	R	29	0	0	66	-4.09
ACC	L	-6	34	18	195	4.21
Cuneus	L	-9	-82	16	301	-4.33
CG2nd						
Ventral Striatum*	R	5	4	-7	13	3.69
TG1st						
dlPFC (BA9)	L	-11	54	34	791	4.49
TG2nd						
Anterior Insula*	L	-40	17	-6	36	3.66
	R	26	23	3	11	3.68
Thalamus*	L	-19	-19	10	2366	-6.99

PPI Seed ROI - Regressor - Region	Laterality	Talairach coordinates			Cluster size	Max stat t
		x	y	z		
Left Ventral Striatum						
CG1st						
Putamen	R	10	10	-1	186	-4.05
dlPFC (BA8)	R	7	34	46	1190	-5.10
CG2nd						
dlPFC (BA9)	R	41	6	39	80	4.05
Lyngual Gyrus	R	23	-79	-3	1354	-5.91
TG1st						
Anterior Insula	L	-31	21	6	357	-4.77
Dorsal ACC	L	-2	20	48	89	-4.04
TG2nd						
Thalamus	L	-12	-32	1	185	-5.43
	R	5	-32	5	191	-4.29
Right Ventral Striatum						
CG1st						
vlPFC	L	-38	16	-5	529	-5.05
CG2nd						
Thalamus	L	-8	-14	2	14	3.86
TG1st						
Anterior Insula	R	39	18	-6	193	-4.71
	L	-37	23	9	25	-3.93
TG2nd						
OFC (BA10)	R	30	50	6	196	-4.48
Dorsal ACC	L	-2	33	47	93	-4.37

Summary of random-effects analyses on PPI regressors (for more details see Methods).
* p<0.05 (activation survives correction for multiple comparisons, FDR corrected for the whole brain volume). Otherwise p<0.006, uncorrected. (BA=Brodmann area)

6 Neural Signatures of Social and Non-Social Outcome Prediction Error, Fairness and Monetary Utility

6.1 Introduction

In choosing the best course of action our brain needs to navigate through a world filled with fundamentally different forms of uncertainty. At times we might be immersed in understanding mere non-social probabilistic reward associations, like when considering our options based on a poker hand. The next moment we might be already predicting the outcomes of a social interaction, like when we need to work out if the other player is bluffing. Given the enormous evolutionary importance of sociality for our species it is plausible that natural selection equipped the human brain with specific mechanisms to deal with social uncertainty. At the same time, the brain might also rely on general mechanisms for motivational control of behaviour that may incorporate both social and non social factors (Ruff & Fehr 2014). For instance mechanisms that keep track of current state and compare it to predictions in order to discover discrepancies that can generate learning.

This is a mechanism that has been widely studied in non-social decision-making by quantitative models of reward processing (Glimcher 2011; Sutton & Barto 1998; Montague et al. 1996). In this context, reinforcement learning represents one of the most successful approaches. Such formal models suggested that processing of uncertain rewards required two signals: a reward prediction and a reward prediction error signal. These theoretical signals were later identified in the neural activity of the primate brain in both single cell recordings and neuroimaging studies (Glimcher 2011; Schultz 2013). Importantly, more recently a similar quantitative approach led to the integration of prediction risk to the theory of reward learning (Preuschoff & Bossaerts 2007). Similarly, this formal framework predicted the existence of two risk-related signals: a risk prediction and a risk prediction error signal. These signals were then identified in the neural activity of the human and primate brain (Preuschoff et al. 2008; d'Acremont et al. 2009; O'Neill & Schultz 2010; O'Neill & Schultz 2013; Rudorf et al. 2012). Interestingly the key structures identified in the human brain reflecting risk prediction and error are the anterior insula, the anterior cingulate cortex (ACC) and the orbitofrontal cortex (OFC).

Social preferences are an important source of uncertainty in human decision-making. A large body of experiments in economics and psychology has shown that people's choice behaviour is critically influenced by consideration of the well being of others, reciprocity and fairness (Camerer 2003). This is in contrast with standard economic models of human decision-making (such as utility theory) that have typically minimised the influence of people's social preferences in decision-making behaviour. Such limitations have been effectively illustrated by empirical findings from a strategic social game known as the ultimatum game. In this game two players are given the opportunity to split a sum of money. One player is assigned the role of proposer and the other of responder. The first player proposes how to divide the sum between the two, and the second player can either accept or reject this proposal. If it is accepted, the money is split as proposed, but if the responder rejects the offer, then neither player receives anything. Contrary to what standard economic models would forecast, that is any monetary amount should be preferable to none, typically offers below 20-30% of the total tend to be rejected despite the fact that such retaliation is costly (Camerer 2003). Neuroimaging studies investigating this effect (Tabibnia et al. 2008; Sanfey et al. 2003; Sanfey 2007) found increased anterior insula and ACC activity in the responders in the contrast between unfair and fair offers. Also, higher insula activity at the time of the offers correlated with subsequent rejection of the offers.

A model of anterior insula's function (Singer et al. 2009) helps in reconciling the findings laid out for non-social risk prediction and error with those on social uncertainty. According to this model anterior insula integrates external sensory and internal physiological signals with computations about their uncertainty, be it social or non-social in nature. This view suggests that anterior insula is a key region where coding of social and non-social reward uncertainty can be directly tested.

To do so, we employed a design where outcome prediction risk and error associated with either a social (trust game) or non-social (card game) gamble were comparable, thus allowing to look for common or distinct neural signatures reflecting equivalent changes in reward uncertainty. Critically, in the social gamble (trust game) we manipulated the fairness of outcomes as well as the associated level of uncertainty.

Given the evidence in favour of a network coding for the fairness of social outcomes (Sanfey et al. 2003; Sanfey 2007) and its overlap with a network previously shown to encode prediction risk and error (Preuschoff et al. 2008; Rudorf et al. 2012), we produced three hypotheses. First, in a direct comparison of social and non-social decision-making, we hypothesised to observe fairness modulations in the same regions coding for risk prediction errors in the non-social domain. Second, we hypothesised fairness modulations to scale with the level of uncertainty resolved as the outcome of the economic game is revealed. Third, we hypothesised to observe modulations due to monetary gains and losses in the non-social but not in the social domain. In fact, the results on the ultimatum game presented above (Sanfey et al. 2003; Sanfey 2007; Tabibnia et al. 2008) do not confirm that the insula is responding to unfairness. Instead the insula could simply be encoding a negative prediction error representing the player's own payoff. To tease apart this alternative explanation, we designed a trust game where fairness and own-payoff are uncorrelated.

6.2 Material and Methods

Here we describe procedures specifically employed for the experiment presented in this chapter focusing on outcome delivery. Whenever there is an overlap with procedures introduced earlier we refer the reader to the methods section of chapter 5.

6.2.1 Participants

A total of 21 healthy participants (11 females, 10 males; mean age, 26.6 years, ±4.82 SD) took part in the study. All participants gave full informed consent to participate in the study. The study was approved by the University of Glasgow Ethics Review Committee.

6.2.2 Experimental task

The experimental task for both card and trust games had 3 steps: betting, outcome anticipation and outcome delivery. In this chapter we focus on outcome delivery (Fig. 6.1; for a complete description of the task see chapter 5 methods section).

6.2.3 fMRI acquisition

(see chapter 5 methods section)

6.2.4 fMRI preprocessing

(see chapter 5 methods section)

6.2.5 fMRI analyses

The statistical analyses of the fMRI data were based on a series of general linear models (GLMs) that can be divided in two parts. For each subject, separate linear models were constructed that included regressors of no interest as well as the regressors described below. Regressors modelled the BOLD response to the specified events using a convolution kernel applied to a boxcar function.

To identify the regions of interests (ROIs) correlated to non-social and social uncertainty parameters we created 2 GLMs. GLM1 included parametric modulations of the card game and trust game regressor: prediction risk (Fig. 5.2; Tab. 5.1). GLM2 included parametric modulations of the card game and trust game regressors: early risk prediction error and late risk prediction error (Preuschoff et al. 2008; Rudorf et al. 2012).

In part 2 of our analysis to illustrate how BOLD activity in the identified regions of interest fitted our model we modified the previous GLMs as follows.

GLMs 3 and 4 were created to extract mean sensitivity values for each reward probability level (Table 6.1) before card 2 (prediction risk) and at card 2 (outcome risk prediction error). GLMs 5 and 6 were created to extract mean sensitivity values and time-course hemodynamic responses for each reward probability level (Table 6.1) after trustee's face was presented before outcome (risk prediction) and at outcome stage (risk prediction error update).

GLM1 and GLM2 were set up to run random effects analyses at the group level to locate the mean beta sensitivities to each regressor of interest. For GLM1 the onset regressor was made of a late long epoch covering the remaining 4 volumes before Card 2 (or outcome coloured square for trust game trials). For GLM2 the onset regressor at Card 2 (or outcome coloured square for trust game trials) was divided in two epochs: an early short epoch of one volume and a late long epoch covering the remaining 4 volumes. Overall the first GLM included the modulating parameter prediction risk during the long epoch before Card 2 (or outcome coloured square for trust game trials). GLM2 included the modulating parameters risk prediction error and outcome (win or loss) at Card 2 (or outcome coloured square for trust game trials).

Contrasts computed for all parametrically modulated regressors were then tested in separate random effects analyses at the group level. We applied a voxelwise statistical threshold of p=0.05 and corrected for multiple comparisons based on False Discovery Rate (FDR) control for the whole-brain volume. Figure 6.2 and Table 6.1 give an overview of the mathematical parameters of interest (for further details on calculation of reward and risk parameters see Appendix I).

To illustrate how the BOLD estimates in our ROIs reflected the hypothesised social and non-social uncertainty modulations we created the following GLMs. In GLM3 the epoch from volume two to five after Card 1 was modelled by ten reward probability regressors. In GLM4 the first volume after Card 2 was modelled by nine separate onset regressors for each risk prediction error value (Table 6.1).

In trust game trials the player's initial choice to trust or not the upcoming trustee generates two sets of conditions (TG-Trust and TG-NoTrust). In GLM5 the epoch from volume two to five after trustee's face was modelled by two sets of six reward probability regressors (one for TG-Trust and one for TG-NoTrust conditions; Table 6.1). In GLM6 the first volume after the coloured square signalling outcome was modelled by two sets of six separate regressors (one for TG-Trust and one for TG-NoTrust conditions) reflecting level of uncertainty, fairness and monetary utility.

Next, we extracted the mean beta estimates for each regressor for each subject, averaged across all subjects and plotted the overall mean estimates (Fig.6.3). For Figure 6.1S card game plots we averaged the first 3, second 3 and last 3 RiPE values, whether for trust game plots we averaged the first 2, second 2 and last 2 outcome prediction error conditions. In so doing the card game and trust game effects become directly comparable.

We also extracted ROIs hemodynamic time-courses at time of outcome delivery (Fig. 6.5) for trust game conditions. For both sets of conditions we plotted three time-courses corresponding to the outcome regressors reflecting level of uncertainty, fairness and monetary utility. Note that in this type of design, unlike in a typical ultimatum game paradigm (Sanfey et al. 2003), the two independent variables fairness of outcomes and monetary utility are uncorrelated. So that both fair and unfair outcomes can lead to either a loss or a win.

TG-Trust conditions (participant bet that trustee will share): (C1) expected fair outcome, low outcome prediction error, monetary win; (C2) unexpected fair and unfair outcome, high outcome prediction error, monetary win and loss; (C3) expected unfair outcome, low outcome prediction error, monetary loss.

TG-NoTrust conditions (participant bet that trustee will not share): (C1) expected fair outcome, low outcome prediction error, monetary loss; (C2) unexpected fair and unfair outcome, high outcome prediction error, monetary win and loss; (C3) expected unfair outcome, low outcome prediction error, monetary win.

Finally to further explore potential sources of interaction between the fairness of the trustee's response and the corresponding outcome in the context of our trust games (TG-Trust and TG-

NoTrust), we used mean beta weights extracted from our ROIs in a repeated-measures 2x2 ANOVA comparing all fair and unfair conditions with gain and no gain outcome conditions.

6.3 Results

We first present the results of the whole brain analyses (GLMs 1 and 2) that focused on the outcome delivery window starting with the prediction of outcome and ending with the onset of the second stimulus (second card or coloured square). We then proceed with the results from the ROI analyses (GLMs 4 and 5 for card game and GLMs 5 and 6 for trust game conditions).

6.3.1 Whole brain parametric analysis of outcome delivery window

In the non-social pure risk domain (card game) the parametric regressor representing prediction risk (PR) correlated with activations in the ventral striatum, caudate head and insula among other regions ($p < 0.001$, uncorrected; see Table 6.2 for the list of areas). In addition, the regressor modulated by outcome RiPE covaried with activation in anterior insula, dorsal anterior cingulate cortex (dACC), dorsolateral prefrontal cortex (dlPFC) and orbitofrontal cortex (OFC) ($p < 0.05$, FDR corrected for the whole brain volume; Table 6.2). Taken together, these results reflecting PR and RiPE signals in the non-social domain are consistent with a number of recent studies (Rudorf et al. 2012; Preuschoff et al. 2006; Preuschoff et al. 2008; Schultz et al. 2008).

In the social domain (trust game) both parametric regressors representing PR and outcome RiPE did not yield significant activations at the threshold set ($p<0.001$ uncorrected). This result was expected for reasons that can be related to the specific design of the outcome phase. Specifically, trustee players previously deemed by the participant as untrustworthy or trustworthy maintain a consistent sharing behaviour in our trust game. This means that the trustee previously judged trustworthy will share and the untrustworthy will not share. The highest uncertainty lies with trustee players previously rated in the middle of the trustworthiness scale. Such a design choice on one hand discarded the most extreme prediction error discrepancies, lowering the power of the whole brain analysis for this regressor. On the other hand it had the advantage to avoid introduction of potential confounds where participants would learn that their social judgements had been violated. Importantly, this design allowed us to investigate the effect of fairness of outcome and how it scaled with the level of uncertainty generated by reward probability conditions. Furthermore, we could directly test how regions coding for non-social uncertainty reflected our social manipulation. We therefore run another whole brain contrast to look for regions that would respond to the fairness of outcome in trust game trials. We found that a network of regions including anterior insula, dorsal ACC and dorsolateral prefrontal cortex (dlPFC) were positively correlated with unfair and negatively correlated with fair outcomes (trust game contrast unfair>fair; $p<0.001$ uncorrected; Tab. 6.3). Interestingly, these are also the same regions found to reflect RiPE in the non-social domain.

Overall these results are interesting because they suggested a direct link, in the context of the same study, between regions found to modulate non-social RiPE with regions reflecting modulation of fairness and uncertainty of outcomes. Such a scenario has been predicted in models of anterior insula function that suggest the integration of uncertainty with bodily, affective and sensory information (Singer et al. 2009), as well as by studies revealing that anterior insula activation precedes the choice to defect against unfair but not fair players (Sanfey et al. 2003). In the following section we further illustrate this experimental question.

6.3.2 Regions of interest analyses

We identified a distinct network of regions processing degrees of non-social uncertainty and fairness of social outcomes in the whole brain analysis. This result further motivated testing of our hypothesis. That is, regions previously found to modulate non-social RiPE would also modulate fairness and such modulation would scale with the uncertainty of outcomes in our trust game.

The outcome RiPE depends on the reward expectation conveyed by the first card or trustee's face, but also on the actual outcome of the gamble. Thus its value varies across trials, allowing to search for an early neural signal at outcome. To test this hypothesis we modified the specifications of our general linear model to compare the corresponding activation of each reward probability condition at outcome within the identified regions of interest.

6.3.3 Activity at outcome in anterior insula and dACC reflects non-social RiPE as well as fairness and uncertainty of social outcomes

In the whole-brain analysis we replicated previous findings (Preuschoff et al. 2008; Rudorf et al. 2012) showing that activity in a distributed network including bilateral anterior insula, dACC and bilateral OFC, covaried with outcome RiPE in the non-social domain ($p < 0.05$, FDR corrected for the whole brain volume; Table 6.2).

To avoid circular inferences we used regions of interest previously found to reflect non-social RiPE during outcome anticipation to illustrate how the response profile in these regions reflected non-social RiPE at outcome. We also illustrate how this activation is reflected in bilateral OFC as found in the whole brain analysis. Concurrently we illustrate how these regions reflected fairness and uncertainty of outcome in the social domain. To do so we plotted mean activation estimates as a function of all RiPE value conditions for card game trials and as a function of fairness of outcome and low/high outcome prediction error (PE) values for trust game trials (Fig. 6.3; see also Fig. 6.1S where card game and trust game effects are more directly comparable).

Similarly to what found in recent studies investigating non-social pure risk (Preuschoff et al. 2008; Rudorf et al. 2012), card game plots show that outcome activity in bilateral anterior insula, dACC ($p<0.05$, FDR corrected for the whole brain volume) following presentation of the second card reflects RiPE when modelled as a linear function of all RiPE values (Fig. 6.3). As expected same patterns were obtained for the regions of interest that passed multiple correction in the whole brain analysis of outcome RiPE (Fig. 6.3 illustrates activity in bilateral OFC).

We then directly compared the patterns of activation for trust game trials in the same regions of interest that reflected modulation of RiPE in the non-social domain. As predicted from the whole brain analysis contrasting unfair and fair outcome responses, activity in bilateral anterior insula and dACC was higher for unfair responses (Fig. 6.3, red markers) and lower for fair responses (green markers). Interestingly the same pattern was observed in bilateral OFC.

Our experimental manipulation (TG-Trust; TG-NoTrust) allows to test whether or not these regions were modulated by monetary gains and losses as it is the case in the non-social domain (Fig. 6.3). Plots show that in the social domain activity in bilateral anterior insula, dACC and bilateral OFC does not reflect monetary utility. Winning and losing trials are both associated with higher BOLD activation in these regions when the outcome is expected unfair, and with lower activation when it is expected fair.

Crucially, plots show that response to fairness scales with the level of uncertainty of the outcome (low/high outcome PE). Low PE conditions are those where the participant is expecting a fair or unfair outcome. Conversely, high PE conditions are those where the participant is more uncertain whether the outcome is going to be fair or unfair. Activity in bilateral anterior insula, dACC and bilateral OFC is modulated by both fairness and uncertainty of the social outcome. To better illustrate this point we plotted combined mean beta estimates of fairness and uncertainty outcome conditions (Fig. 6.4). Plots show not only a modulation due to the fairness of outcome, but also a differentiation between low and high outcome PE.

We also tested the effect of the fairness dimension on the outcome dimension of the trust games. When betting on Trust the player will win when receiving a fair response from the trustee and lose when faced with an unfair response. When in turn the player plays NoTrust then he will win when faced with an unfair response from the trustee and lose when faced with a fair one. To further explore this counterintuitive relation between the fairness of the trustee responses on a given trial and the corresponding type of outcome associated in the No-Trust conditions (as compared to the Trust conditions), we used mean beta weights extracted from our ROIs in a repeated-measures ANOVA that probed the interaction between level of fairness (low or high) and level of reward (low or high). The interaction did not reach significance in all regions (anterior insula: $F(1,19)=2.8$, $P=0.11$; dACC: $F(1,19)=0.002$, $P=0.96$; OFC $F(1,19)=0.20$, $P=0.66$).

Finally, we produced time-course hemodynamic responses to fairness of outcome, level of uncertainty and monetary utility (Fig. 6.5). Regardless of the participant's monetary gain bilateral anterior insula, dACC and bilateral OFC activation is higher for trustee unfair responses and lower for fair responses (outcome PE low). The blue dotted line shows modulation of fair and unfair conditions associated with high outcome PE, thus representing uncertainty differentiation.

We also plotted the combined activity of outcome anticipation and outcome delivery windows for bilateral anterior insula and dACC (Fig. 6.6). Here in addition to the modulation of fairness and uncertainty at outcome, one can see the corresponding initial reward prediction error modulation after presentation of trustee's face (for more details on outcome anticipation see the study presented in chapter 5, Fig.5.3). Note that neural activation during outcome anticipation for TG-Trust and NoTrust trials is lower at onset for low RePE and higher for high RePE regardless of the expected fairness of trustee (i.e. regardless of the trustee been trustworthy or untrustworthy). At outcome delivery this tendency is inverted. Here neural activation for both TG Trust and NoTrust conditions is always higher when trustee's answer is unfair (red) and lower when it is fair (green), regardless of the actual outcome and monetary gain.

6.4 Discussion

In this study we first compared activation patterns associated with prediction risk and risk prediction error (RiPE) during the outcome phase of two types of gambles: a card game manipulating non-social uncertainty, and a trust game manipulating social uncertainty. We then investigated whether regions coding for non-social RiPE reflected also modulation of fairness of outcomes and how this scaled with level of reward uncertainty and monetary utility.

In the trust betting game reward uncertainty varied along a social dimension (trustworthiness). In the card game (Preuschoff et al. 2006) reward uncertainty varied along a non-social dimension (pure risk). The trust game maintained the same structure of the card game so that the social and non-social dimensions could be compared on a similar scale.

To locate regions distinctively responding to either social or non-social modulations of outcome prediction risk and error we run whole brain analyses (Table 6.2). Based on previous work (Sanfey et al. 2003) we also run contrast analyses to locate regions responding to fairness of outcomes (Table 6.3). Results from this first set of analyses supported one of our predictions, that similar brain regions would represent non-social RiPE and fairness of outcome in the social domain.

This result further motivated testing of our hypotheses. We then set up region of interest analyses to illustrate whether regions found to modulate non-social RiPE in the card game, would also modulate fairness and outcome prediction error in our trust game. We found that activity in the same clusters of bilateral anterior insula, dACC and bilateral OFC reflected modulation of non-social RiPE as well as fairness and level of reward uncertainty of social outcomes (Fig. 6.3, 6.4). In addition we found that activation due to fairness in these regions is not modulated by monetary gains and losses (Fig. 6.5).

6.4.1 Anterior insula, dACC and OFC activity reflects non-social RiPE as well as modulation of fairness and uncertainty of social outcomes

Recent models accounting for the variety of functions attributed to anterior insula suggest that this structure of the human brain is responsible for the integration of uncertainty with bodily, affective and sensory information (Singer et al. 2009; Craig 2009). Such activity in turn would support learning as well as physiological reactions in decision-making under risk.

124

Anterior insula is situated between subcortical and higher cortical areas and is anatomically interconnected to both sites, placing it in an ideal position for higher level integration of feeling states. Singer and colleagues (Singer et al. 2009) proposed a model of anterior insular cortex where predictive feeling states are integrated with current feeling states and feeling state prediction errors. One important aspect of this model is that it supports error-based learning of feeling states in insula related to both social and non-social sources of uncertainty. Such a view critically rests on a number of studies providing evidence in favour of the specific role played by anterior insula in processing uncertainty, and in particular risk prediction and error. One example in the context of non-social decision-making is the work of Preuschoff and colleagues (2008). Using a gambling task manipulating pure risk they found that activity in bilateral anterior insula computed risk prediction when waiting for the outcome of a risky decision. Later in time activity in the same region reflected risk prediction error once the outcome was revealed. Thus, in the non-social domain of risky decision-making, anterior insula could be the centre where predicted risk is compared to realised risk. In the social domain of risky decision-making, Sanfey and colleagues (2003) showed that anterior insula activation precedes the choice to defect against unfair but not fair players. The study found also that, in the ultimatum game, the responder's perception of fairness of the offer was reflected by both anterior insula and ACC activity. Notably, anterior insula activation was scaled monotonically with fairness of offers: higher for more unfair and lower for fairer offers. Anterior insula and ACC are often reported jointly activated in fMRI studies. This is consistent with the idea that these regions serve as complementary limbic sensory and motor regions that work together (Craig 2009).

Recently, in the context of non-social decision-making it has been proposed that the orbitofrontal cortex (OFC) could signal prediction errors. This observation has been replicated using monkey's single neuron recordings as well as in human fMRI experiments (Stalnaker et al. 2015). On the other hand, in social settings BOLD activity in OFC has been shown to reflect fairness of outcomes (fair>unfair) in experiments using the ultimatum game (Tabibnia et al. 2008). Taken together these results suggest a model of OFC coding for social and non-social forms of uncertainty using a common neural scale.

Our data are consistent with the model laid out of anterior insula's function and suggest that two key regions of integration could be dACC and OFC. Indeed we found that, as predicted by the model (Singer et al. 2009) activity in anterior insula not only reflects risk prediction and errors in the non-social domain, but also modulation of fairness of outcomes (Fig. 6.3). A similar activation profile was found in dACC and bilateral OFC. Importantly, we noted that previous studies (Sanfey et al. 2003) found that anterior insula and dACC activity scaled monotonically with fairness of offers. Our data show that activity in these regions also scales with level of uncertainty when fairness of outcomes is more or less expected (low/high outcome prediction error; Fig. 6.4).

This result is noteworthy as it provides direct evidence, in the context of the same study, of how the brain processes social and non-social decision-making within the same neural substrates. Two main theories have been proposed to explain how the brain might encode reward uncertainty representations underlying social and non-social choices (Ruff & Fehr 2014). One theory assumes that the brain dedicates largely separate networks for encoding social and non-social forms of uncertainty and for assigning value to different choice alternatives. In contrast, a second theory proposes that the same network processes different forms of uncertainty and converts the values associated with different choice alternatives into a common neural scale. Our results show that indeed the same network of regions processes fundamentally distinct forms of uncertainty: non-social RiPE on one hand and fairness and outcome prediction error on the other. Intriguingly, besides this element of convergence we found also an element of divergence from a common neural scale model.

6.4.2 Anterior insula, dACC and OFC activity reflects fairness of outcomes but not monetary utility

In the social domain, activation due to fairness in anterior insula, dACC and OFC is not modulated by monetary gains and losses (Fig. 6.5). Activation to unfair outcomes is higher than that to fair outcomes when this is associated with monetary losses, as well as when it is associated to wins. This is a surprising result considering that, in the context of the same experiment, these regions are indeed modulated by the actual gains and losses in the non-social domain (Fig. 6.3). In particular in the card game (non-social) expected losses and wins are always associated with the same level of activation representing same level of prediction error. Crucially, our trust game design allows to test whether modulation of the regions of interest is correlated to fairness of outcome or monetary utility. In fact, participants' initial bet (to decide whether the upcoming partner will share or not at the start of the trust game) generates two sets of conditions where fairness and monetary utility become uncorrelated (TG-Trust and TG-NoTrust). In TG-Trust trials unfair outcomes always lead to a loss and a fair outcome to a win. On the contrary, in TG-NoTrust trials unfair outcomes always lead to a win and fair outcome to a loss. Therefore monetary wins (and losses) are associated alternatively to both fair and unfair outcomes. Such a design overcomes the limits of a typical ultimatum game, as in (Sanfey et al. 2003) where normally unfair offers result in less money for the responder, implying that if we observe brain activity that correlates with smaller offers, then it is unclear how much of this activity is due to perceived unfairness and how much is simply due to earning less money.

We found that regardless of the outcome being associated with wins or losses activation to unfair trustees' responses is always higher than that associated with fair responses. This finding is noteworthy as it replicates previous findings showing modulation to fairness in anterior insula, while ruling out the effect of own payoff as a potential confounding factor.

One possible interpretation of this finding is that this network of regions prioritises resolution of uncertainty related to fairness behaviour over tracking of actual gains and losses. Notably, this mechanism resembles the behaviour of the responder in the ultimatum game prioritising fairness motives over immediate gains and rational maximisation of outcomes (Sanfey et al. 2003; Sanfey 2007). In this sense the observed neural signature might constitute one of the key steps in the neural cascade leading to the primacy of moral over rational decision-making reported in behaviour (Camerer 2003). One hypothesis is that the observed neural modulation might serve the function of weighting fairness to inform behavioural choice. Highest activity in this network might signal highest certainty of perceived unfairness. Conversely, lowest activity might signal highest certainty of perceived fairness. As uncertainty becomes larger the two opposite signals converge at the highest risk point, where weighting of fairness is most uncertain (Fig. 6.3). Further experimentation could test whether this weighting signal is predictive of future behaviour (e.g. amount of financial investments changing as a function of the preceding activity related to the weighting of fairness uncertainty). An aspect here not addressed is the influence to and from other regions. Further experimentation using connectivity analysis or causal designs (as in Knoch and colleagues 2006 TMS study) might further reveal the involvement of regions such as dlPFC in regulating the mismatch between social and non-social utility maximisation, and how this is translated in choice behaviour.

6.4.3 Conclusion

Importantly, we were able to compare the form brain activity takes when processing prediction errors and outcome reward in non-social pure risk and social decision-making situations. As expected in the non-social domain outcome risk prediction errors were represented in a network of regions including anterior insula, dACC and OFC as a function of the mathematical uncertainty and the actual wins and losses that resolved it. Crucially, we found that the same regions responded to our trust game social manipulation. BOLD activity was modulated by both fairness and uncertainty of outcomes, but independently of actual gains and losses. On one hand these results speak in favour of a common neural scale used by the brain when processing social and non-social risky decision-making. On the other hand, this study provides also evidence of distinct neural processes involved in resolving uncertainty when fairness and monetary rewards are involved. More generally these observations indicate that further research is needed to better characterise the neural processes underlying the interplay between moral and rational, self-interested decision-making.

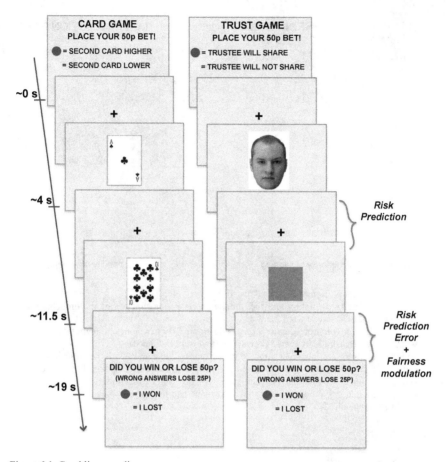

Figure 6.1. Gambling paradigm.

Participants played card game (CG) and trust game (TG) trials presented in random order. In card game trials they first bet on the second card presented being higher or lower than the first one. In trust game trials they bet on whether the trustee associated to that game was going to return a share or not. The timeline of the two types of gamble is identical. After placing their bet participants watch the first card or trustee's face followed 7.5s later by a second card or a coloured square revealing the outcome of the gamble (green=trustee shared; red=trustee kept). Finally participants were asked to confirm if they won or lost on that gamble.

Before display of the outcome a risk prediction update occurs. A final risk prediction error update occurs at outcome after display of second card or a coloured square, when the gamble is resolved.

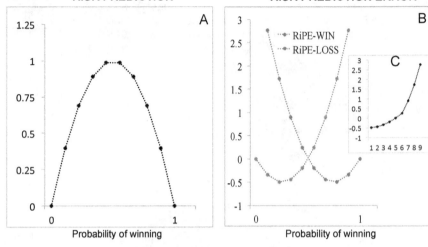

Figure 6.2. Decision parameters functions.
Plots illustrate risk prediction and risk prediction error as a function of the probability of winning before and after display of Card 2.
Before Card 2 (or coloured square) is revealed risk prediction becomes a function of the probability of winning and is quadratic in reward probability (inversely U-shaped).
At outcome after Card 2 is revealed the error becomes a function of both the probability of winning at Card 1 and the actual win or loss. Therefore the risk prediction error update (B) is represented by two symmetric functions that can be summarised in one single function (C) with nine values each representing one risk prediction error level for wins and the corresponding one for losses (for more details see Appendix I).

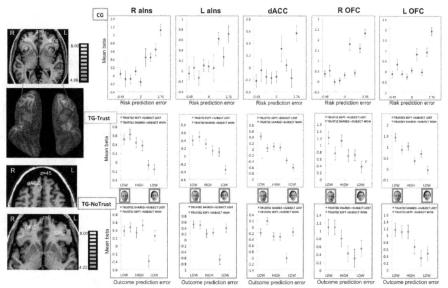

Figure 6.3. Activity in anterior insula, dACC and OFC reflects modulation of outcome fairness and uncertainty.

Figures (from top left: axial, bilateral inflated cortex and axial view) show statistical parametric maps of the random effects analysis colour coded for the t-values ($p<0.05$, FDR corrected for the whole brain volume, $df=19$).

First row plots (CG) show that neural activation in bilateral anterior insula (aIns), dorsal anterior cingulate cortex (dACC) and orbitofrontal cortex (OFC) to card game trials at outcome correlates positively with risk prediction error after second card. This second prediction error update is represented as a linear function of all possible risk prediction error values (see Methods). Activation in the same regions to both trust game subgroups of conditions (TG-Trust; TG-No trust) correlates with trustee's fairness and it scales linearly with outcome prediction error (high/low). As the outcome prediction error increases activity to trustee fairness increases (green markers), whether activation to trustee unfairness decreases (red markers). Importantly, card game plots show modulation to monetary wins and loses at outcome (CG). The same is not true for trust game plots that show no modulation due to monetary utility. Error bars=SE.

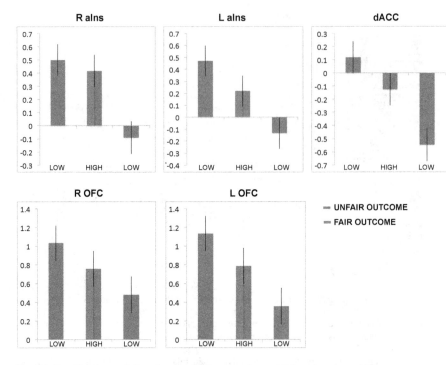

Fig. 6.4. Combined mean beta estimates of fairness and uncertainty outcome conditions.
Bar plots show the combined activity (y-axis, mean beta) in bilateral anterior insula (aIns), dorsal anterior cingulate cortex (dACC) and bilateral orbitofrontal cortex (OFC) for both trust game subgroup of conditions (TG-Trust; TG-NoTrust) to fairness of outcome and outcome prediction error level (x-axis, low/high PE). Expected unfair and fair outcomes (low PE) are reflected in highest and lowest activity. Note neural differentiation of unfair and fair unexpected outcomes (high PE, red and green bar). Error bars=SE.

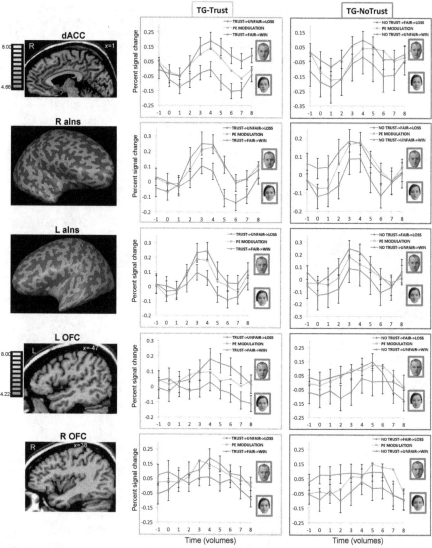

Figure 6.5. Social modulation to level of fairness, uncertainty and monetary reward at outcome.

Figures (from top left: sagittal view, right and left inflated cortex and sagittal view) show statistical parametric maps of the random effects analysis colour coded for the t-values (p<0.05, FDR corrected for the whole brain volume, df=19).

Event-related plots show the corresponding time-course activity in each region of interest to trustee expected unfair (red line) and fair (green line) responses, outcome prediction error level (PE low) and the associated monetary reward: winning (green triangles) and losing (red circles). Blue dashed line represents the average of the unexpected fair and unfair conditions associated with high outcome prediction error.

Neural activation in bilateral anterior insula (aIns), dorsal anterior cingulate cortex (dACC) and bilateral orbitofrontal cortex (OFC) to trust game gambles is higher for unfair conditions (trustee kept) compared to fair conditions (trustee shared). Plots also show modulation due to high outcome PE (blue line). Note also that there is no modulation due to monetary wins and losses. Regardless of the participant's monetary gain activity is higher for trustee's unfair responses and lower for fair responses.

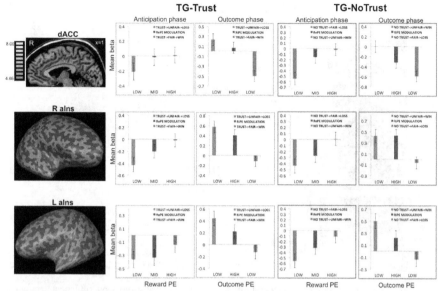

Figure 6.6. Bar plots comparing activations during anticipation phase with outcome delivery phase.
Figures (from top left: sagittal view, right and left inflated cortex) show statistical parametric maps of the random effects analysis colour coded for the t-values (p<0.05, FDR corrected for the whole brain volume, df=19).

Bar plots show the corresponding activity in each region of interest due to initial presentation of trustee's face (anticipation phase) and to outcome delivery (outcome phase).

Neural activation in bilateral anterior insula (aIns) and dorsal anterior cingulate cortex (dACC) during outcome anticipation for TG-Trust and NoTrust trials is lower at onset for low RePE and higher for high RePE regardless of the expected fairness of trustee.

At outcome delivery this tendency is inverted. Here neural activation for both TG Trust and NoTrust conditions is higher when trustee's answer is unfair (red) and lower when it is fair (green), regardless of the actual outcome and monetary gain.

135

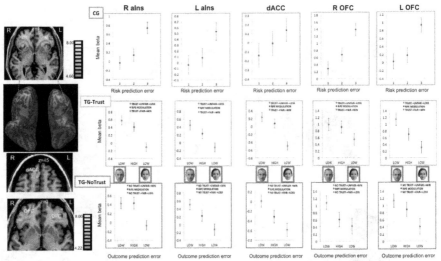

Figure 6.1S. Activity in anterior insula, dACC and OFC reflects modulation of outcome fairness and uncertainty.

Figures (from top left: axial, bilateral inflated cortex and axial view) show statistical parametric maps of the random effects analysis colour coded for the t-values (p<0.05, FDR corrected for the whole brain volume, df=19).

First row plots (CG) show that neural activation in bilateral anterior insula (aIns), dorsal anterior cingulate cortex (dACC) and orbitofrontal cortex (OFC) to card game trials at outcome correlates positively with risk prediction error after second card. This second prediction error update is represented as a linear function of the 3 bins of risk prediction error values (see Methods). Activation in the same regions to both trust game subgroups of conditions (TG-Trust; TG-No trust) correlates with trustee's fairness and it scales linearly with outcome prediction error (high/low). As the outcome prediction error increases activity to trustee fairness increases (green markers), whether activation to trustee unfairness decreases (red markers). Importantly, card game plots show modulation to monetary wins and loses at outcome (CG). The same is not true for trust game plots that show no modulation due to monetary utility. Error bars=SE.

136

Table 6.1. Card game and trust game decision parameters values.

Reward Probability at Card 1 (p)	PR	RiPE-Win	RiPE-Loss
0*	0		0
0.11*	0.40	2.76	-0.34
0.22	0.69	1.73	-0.49
0.33	0.89	0.89	-0.44
0.44**	0.99	0.25	-0.20
0.56**	0.99	-0.20	0.25
0.67	0.89	-0.44	0.89
0.78	0.69	-0.49	1.73
0.89***	0.40	-0.34	2.76
1***	0	0	

The table shows all decision parameter values for risk prediction (PR) and risk prediction error before Card 2 at Card 2 (RiPE-Win and RiPE-Loss) corresponding to each initial reward probability condition at Card 1 (mathematical details can be found in Appendix I).
*Corresponding values for low reward probability in trust game trials.
**Corresponding values for mid reward probability in trust game trials.
***Corresponding values for high reward probability in trust game trials.

Table 6.2. Regions positively correlated with non-social uncertainty parameters at outcome (card game).

Region	Laterality	Talairach coordinates			Cluster size	Max stat t
		x	y	z		
Prediction risk						
Ventral striatum	L	-10	0	-8	245	3.48
Caudate head	L/R	-3	14	0	847	3.18
Midbrain	L	-10	-12	-20	90	2.95
Anterior cingulate cortex	L	-11	29	-6	110	3.38
Insula	R	33	-3	16	258	3.82
Risk prediction error						
Anterior insula	R	41	13	-8	76	4.83*
	L	-32	15	-6	241	6.02*
Dorsal ACC	R/L	-5	30	50	278	6.14*
Medial frontal gyrus/dlPFC	L	-6	42	28	667	6.25*
Inferior frontal gyrus/OFC	R	43	34	-1	2260	7.41*
	L	-47	33	0	2107	6.89*
Midbrain (substantia nigra)	L	-5	-14	-14	39	5.12*

Summary of random-effect analyses (for more details see Methods).
* $p < 0.05$ (activation survives correction for multiple comparisons, FDR corrected for the whole brain volume). Otherwise $p < 0.001$, uncorrected.

Table 6.3. Regions positively correlated with unfair and negatively correlated with fair outcomes (trust game contrast unfair>fair).

Region	Laterality	x	y	z	Cluster size	Max stat t
		Talairach coordinates				
Anterior insula	R	32	26	4	169	3.50
	L	-37	21	4	214	3.69
Dorsal ACC	L	-4	26	43	164	3.42
Inferior FG/vlPFC	L	-55	20	7	452	3.75
Medial frontal gyrus/dlPFC	R	47	28	34	275	3.70
	L	-52	19	25	768	3.90
Middle temporal gyrus	L	-46	-29	-2	1679	4.42
Midbrain	L/R	-1	-16	-20	1724	4.53

p<0.001 (uncorrected).

7 Neural correlates of Motivational Prediction Errors in Primary Visual Area V1

7.1 Introduction

Theories attempting to uncover general mechanisms of brain's function have long proposed its role in creating an internal generative model of the world that embodies predictions of what should be expected. For instance, Helmholtz viewed perception as the generation of inferences about the state of the world, given the sensory data collected (von Helmholtz 1867). Contemporary predictive coding models support the notion that coding of prediction errors is a general neural coding strategy throughout the brain (Friston 2005; Clark 2013).

In general a prediction error can be seen as the discrepancy between prior expectations and new information acquired about the state of the world. The agent's model of the world is partly hard-wired in the structure of neural circuits and partly derived from the sensory inputs experienced. In this sense, a prediction error signals some form of mismatch between the current evidence and what is predicted based on the current internal model, and importantly, calls for an update.

Coding of prediction errors has been observed throughout the brain, in relation to the processing of sensory signals, value, motor actions, and cognitive control (den Ouden et al. 2012). In this context, a useful distinction is that between unsigned and signed prediction errors. Prediction errors that reflect simply the level of surprise, are often referred to as unsigned. However, in order to use prediction errors to guide motivational decision-making, not only the size but also its valence (sign) has to be conveyed. Signed prediction errors therefore signal also whether an outcome was better or worse than expected in a motivational sense. Perceptual prediction errors are typically unsigned whether motivational prediction errors are typically signed.

Predictive coding models (Rao & Ballard 1999; Friston 2005; Spratling 2008) offer a possible mechanism that can be tested where at the centre are prediction and prediction error units. This has been proposed for the cortical column, considered by these models the basic computational module. But recent experiments show how even in subcortical structures a similar mechanism of feedback predictions and feedforward inputs can give rise to prediction errors (Cohen et al. 2012). The same mechanism therefore might be used in regions typically associated with the generation of perceptual prediction errors (in early visual areas) and the generation of motivational predictions errors (in subcortical dopaminergic structures).

We know today that human primary visual cortex is not just a passive transformer of sensory inputs. Rather, activity in early visual areas is influenced by attention, task, training and expectation (Gilbert & Sigman 2007; Muckli 2010). This is reflected in the fact that even V1, the first most important cortical station in the visual pathway, receives considerably more feedback and lateral input than feedforward thalamic connections (Budd 1998). The understanding of such rich feedback mechanisms to V1 is crucial for a more global understanding of early visual areas and more in general macrocircuit communication (Muckli & Petro 2013).

In a previous functional connectivity analysis we found that a region of the prefrontal cortex coding for social and non-social motivational prediction errors influenced early visual areas (Fig. 5.7). Given the fact that unsigned prediction errors have been found in regions thought to code only motivational prediction errors [primate midbrain, (Matsumoto & Hikosaka 2009); human striatum, (Zink et al. 2003), (den Ouden et al. 2010); and ventral tegmental area, (Bunzeck & Düzel 2006)], we hypothesised that signed prediction errors could be found in early visual areas.

To answer these questions we run a retinotopic experiment on a subgroup of participants that took part in a previous study and identified V1 visual areas. We then tested, using results from a card game (non-social) and a trust game (social), whether activity in early visual areas reflected motivational prediction errors (as found in the previous study for other cortical and subcortical areas, Fig. 5.3). We also further tested whether social and non-social degrees of uncertainty were processed according to a common neural scale model (Ruff & Fehr 2014).

7.2 Material and Methods

Here we describe procedures specifically employed for the experiment presented in this chapter on outcome anticipation and delivery in early visual areas. Whenever there is an overlap with procedures introduced earlier we refer the reader to the methods section of chapter 5.

7.2.1 Participants

A total of 12 healthy participants (6 females, 6 males; mean age, 27.75 years, ±5.35 SD) took part in the study. All participants gave full informed consent to participate in the study. The study was approved by the University of Glasgow Ethics Review Committee.

7.2.2 Experimental task

The experimental procedure for the retinotopic mapping experiment is presented below in the dedicated section.

The experimental task for both card and trust games had 3 steps: betting, outcome anticipation and outcome delivery. In this study we focus on both outcome anticipation and outcome delivery phases (see Fig. 7.1; for a complete description of the task see chapter 5 methods section).

7.2.3 fMRI acquisition

(see chapter 5 methods section)

7.2.4 fMRI preprocessing

(see chapter 5 methods section)

7.2.5 fMRI analyses

Here we describe the GLMs used for the parametric analyses of the outcome anticipation and outcome delivery phases.

The statistical analyses of the fMRI data were based on a series of general linear models (GLMs) that can be divided in two parts. For each subject, separate linear models were constructed that included regressors of no interest as well as the regressors described below. Regressors modelled the BOLD response to the specified events using a convolution kernel applied to a boxcar function.

In part 1, to identify the regions of interests (ROIs) correlated to non-social and social uncertainty parameters we created 3 GLMs. GLM1 included parametric modulations of the card game and trust game regressors: reward prediction error 1 (RePE1) and subsequent risk prediction (PR; Table 7.1). GLM2 included parametric modulations of the card game and trust game regressors: risk prediction error 1 (RiPE1) and late reward prediction error. GLM3 included parametric modulations of the card game and trust game regressors: risk prediction error 2 and late risk prediction error 2 (Preuschoff et al. 2006; Preuschoff et al. 2008; Rudorf et al. 2012).

In part 2 of our analysis to illustrate how BOLD activity in the identified regions of interest fitted our computational model we modified the previous GLMs as follows. GLM4 was created to extract mean sensitivity values for each reward probability level at card 1 (first risk and reward prediction error update; Fig. 7.3 and 7.4). GLM5 was created to extract mean sensitivity values for each reward probability level after trustee's face was presented (first reward prediction error update; Fig. 7.3 and 7.4).

GLM1, GLM2 and GLM3 were set up to run fixed effects analyses at the single subject and group level to locate the mean beta sensitivities to each regressor of interest. For GLM1 and GLM2 the onset regressor at Card 1 (or trustee's face) was divided in two epochs: an early short epoch of one volume and a late long epoch of about 4 volumes depending on the jittered interval until the onset of Card 2 (or outcome coloured square for trust game conditions). For GLM3 the onset regressor at Card 2 (or outcome coloured square for TG) was divided in two epochs: an early short epoch of one volume and a late long epoch covering the remaining 4 volumes. Overall the first two GLMs included the modulating parameters expected reward and risk prediction error at onset of Card 1 (or trustee's face) and risk prediction during the long epoch before Card 2 (or outcome coloured square for TG). GLM3 included the modulating parameters risk prediction error and outcome (win or loss) at Card 2 (or outcome coloured square for TG).

Contrasts computed for all parametrically modulated regressors were then tested in separate fixed effects analyses at single subject and group level (Supplementary figure 7.1S and Table 7.1 give an overview of the mathematical parameters of interest. For further details on calculation of reward and risk parameters see Appendix I).

To illustrate how the BOLD estimates in the identified ROIs reflected the hypothesised social and non-social uncertainty modulations we created the following GLMs. In GLM4 the first volume after Card 1 was modelled by ten reward probability regressors. In trust game trials the player's initial choice to trust or not the upcoming trustee generates two sets of conditions (TG-Trust and TG-NoTrust) where economic uncertainty and trustworthiness become orthogonal variables. In GLM5 the first volume after trustee's face was modelled by two sets of six reward probability (Table 7.1) regressors (one for TG-Trust and one for TG-NoTrust conditions). Next, we extracted the mean beta estimates for each regressor for each participant, averaged across all subjects and plotted the overall mean estimates (Fig. 7.3, 7.4). Card game plots for Fig.7.4 (bottom plots) and supplementary figure 7.2S were obtained by averaging the first 3, middle 4 and last 3 reward probability values, whether for trust game plots we averaged the first 2, second 2 and last 2 reward probability values. In so doing the card game and trust game effects become directly comparable.

Finally to further explore potential sources of interaction between the trustworthiness of the trustee's face and the corresponding level of reward probability in the context of our trust games (TG-Trust and TG-NoTrust), we used mean beta weights extracted from our ROIs in a repeated-measures 2x2 ANOVA comparing high and low trustworthy faces (excluding the neutral bin) with high and low reward probability (excluding the mid RePE bin).

7.2.6 Retinotopic mapping and V1 analysis

Retinotopic maps are based on topography-preserving projections from the retina to the lateral geniculate nucleus layers (LGN) and from these layers to primary visual area V1. Retinotopic maps can be calculated because the mapping from the retina to the primary visual cortex is topographical and because the early visual areas retain this retinal topography. Using fMRI and appropriate visual stimuli, early visual areas can be mapped in individual human brains (Sereno et al. 1995; Wandell & Winawer 2011).

Here we mapped primary visual areas V1 in a subgroup of 12 participants (6 female) that participated in the experiment presented in chapter 5. We run a phase-encoding experiment where stimulation of the visual field is repeatedly performed and the response to a specific polar angle corresponds to the phase (relative time point) within a cycle (Fig. 7.2).

A phase-encoded retinotopic mapping was run for each participant which included mapping of polar angle. The checkerboard pattern stimulation consisted of a ray-shaped disk segment subtending 22.5 degrees of polar angle. The ray started at the right horizontal meridian and slowly rotated clockwise for a full cycle of 360 degrees within 96 s. Each mapping experiment consisted of ten repetitions of the rotation, with each cycle lasting for 64 s.

To map visual space to corresponding regions in the visual cortex, we used cross-correlation analysis identifying the time point (lag) at which a region responds maximally. We used the predicted hemodynamic signal time course for the first 1/8 of a stimulation cycle (corresponding to 45 degrees visual angle in the polar mapping experiment) and shifted this reference function successively in time (Muckli et al. 2005). Sites activated at particular polar angles were identified through selecting the lag value that resulted in the highest cross-correlation value for a particular voxel. The obtained lag values at particular voxels were encoded in pseudo-colour on corresponding surface patches (triangles) of the reconstructed cortical sheet. Based on the polar-angle mapping experiment, the boundaries of retinotopic cortical areas V1 were estimated manually on the inflated cortical surface of each participant.

Once identified all bilateral cortical areas V1 for each of the 12 participants we run parametric analyses to illustrate whether activity in primary visual areas reflected modulation of social and non-social uncertainty.

We first run region of interest (ROI) analyses where we tested our parametric models for every subject's V1 separately. We tested for parametric modulations using GLMs1-2 (modified to include only the 12 participants of this study). When a parametric predictor yielded significant results we used GLMs3-6 to illustrate how the BOLD estimates in our ROIs reflected the hypothesised social and non-social uncertainty modulations at the group level (12 participants). In figure 7.3 we used 5 probability conditions to illustrate card game effects (each being the average of two consecutive probability conditions starting with $p=0/9$ and $p=1/9$ conditions, up to $p=8/9$ and $p=9/9$ conditions).

In a different set of analyses we created a new VOI (volume of interest) that was the product of the overlap of all the 12 V1-ROIs. We then used this new VOI to identify subregions within the primary visual areas that would respond to the parametric analyses (GLMs1-2). We then used GLMs3-6 to illustrate how the BOLD estimates in the identified subregions reflected the hypothesised social and non-social uncertainty modulations. Figure 7.4 shows the group mean beta estimates for all 12 participants.

7.3 Results

To study whether activity in primary visual areas reflected modulation of social and non-social uncertainty we first determined the extent and borders of early visual area V1 in a retinotopic mapping experiment.

We first present results of the analyses where all participants' V1 areas were tested separately for parametric effects during outcome anticipation and outcome delivery phases. We then turn to the results of the analyses where we tested for subregions responding to our parametric model using a volume of interest (VOI) that included all participants V1 areas combined.

7.3.1 Early activation during outcome anticipation in V1 primary visual cortex reflects modulation of social and non-social uncertainty

We previously noted that information about the outcome of the gamble does not vary at time of bet's decision. Therefore between placing the bet and seeing the first stimulus (either a card or trustee's face) risk prediction remains constant across all trials. The hypothesised uncertainty modulations occur between the first stimulus and the following outcome. Thus, reward prediction error (RePE1) and risk prediction error updates (RiPE1) depend on the first card or trustee's face and vary across trials, allowing to look for a corresponding neural signal. The second risk prediction error update (RiPE2) depends on the reward expectation conveyed by the first card or trustee's face, but also on the outcome of the gamble. Thus its value varies across trials, allowing to search for an early neural signal at outcome. To test this hypothesis we modified the specifications of our general linear models to compare the activation of each reward probability condition within our ROIs identified in a retinotopic mapping experiment (Fig.7.3).

Overall activation of individually defined V1 areas was correlated only with the parametric predictor modelling reward prediction error (RePE1) in both social and non-social domain (CG: $t = 2.15$, $p<0.03$; TG: $t = 3.81$, $p<0.0001$). Figure 7.3 plots (and Fig. 7.2S) illustrate mean activation estimates as a function of all possible probability of winning conditions for both card game (CG) and trust game (TG) gambles and were generated for descriptive purposes. Similarly to what found in other cortical (anterior insula and dorsal anterior cingulate cortex; Fig.5.3, TG) and subcortical regions (ventral striatum, Fig. 5.4 both CG and

148

TG; and amygdala, Fig. 5.5 only TG), activity in V1 increased linearly in the probability of winning.

We also tested the effect of the trustworthiness dimension on the reward expectation dimension of the trust games. As we reported earlier (Chapter 5) when betting on Trust one can expect to win when faced with a trustworthy trustee and to lose when faced with one judged untrustworthy. When in turn one plays NoTrust then he should expect to win when faced with an untrustworthy trustee and expect to lose when faced with one judged trustworthy. To further explore this counterintuitive relation between the trustworthiness of the trustee's face on a given trial and the corresponding level of reward probability associated in the No-Trust conditions (as compared to the Trust conditions), we used mean beta weights extracted from our V1 ROIs in a repeated-measures ANOVA that probed the interaction between level of trustworthiness (low or high) and level of reward probability (low or high). The interaction did not reach significance ($F(1,11)=0.75$, $P=0.40$).

7.3.2 Early activation during outcome anticipation in a subregion of the cuneus reflects differential modulations of social and non-social uncertainty

Functional connectivity analyses reported here in an earlier study showed that a region of the dorsal anterior cingulate cortex (dACC) reflecting differential modulation of social and non-social uncertainty (Fig. 5.3) influenced a target region in the cuneus (Fig. 5.6). This led us to hypothesise that subregions of the cuneus would respond similarly to the parametric model reflected in dACC activity during outcome anticipation.

To test for subregions within the identified V1 areas responding to our models of expected reward and risk we first run GLMs 1, 2 and 3 at a subject level. We did not find significant activations at the statistical threshold set ($p<0.001$ uncorrected). We then created a single VOI (volume of interest mask) from the overlapping of the twelve V1 regions previously identified and proceeded with a region of interest analysis including all 12 participants. We run fixed effects GLMs 1, 2 and 3 and found that a subregion of the cuneus (250 voxels) reflected the hypothesised differential modulation of social and non-social uncertainty during outcome anticipation found in dACC.

To directly illustrate how the response profile in this cluster reflected modulation of uncertainty, we run GMLs 4 and 5 and plotted mean activation estimates as a function of all possible probability of winning conditions for both card game (CG) and trust game (TG) gambles (Fig. 7.4).

This cluster of the cuneus responded to the parametric predictor modelling RiPE1 in the non-social domain (card game trials; p<0.001 uncorrected) and to the parametric predictor modelling RePE1 in the social domain (trust game trials; p<0.001 uncorrected). This is the same differential modulation we observed in a network including bilateral anterior insula and dACC (Fig. 5.3). The cluster observed here is more ventral (x=-12; y=-72; z=22) compared to the one identified in the connectivity analysis between dACC and cuneus (x=0; y=-77; z=31). However, the connectivity analysis cluster partially overlaps with the VOI mask of the 12 combined V1 areas (light blue mask over dark blue in bottom right, Fig. 7.4).

These findings suggest that though the overall activity in V1 correlates with early outcome anticipation in the form of a reward prediction error signal (RePE1), at a more local level there are clusters responding to the discrepancy between RePE1 and its expected value, namely, risk prediction error (RiPE1). It is striking to observe - though the cluster found did not pass correction for multiple comparisons - that activity in a region of the early visual cortex would reflect differential modulations of social and non-social uncertainty as predicted by a previously performed functional connectivity analysis.

We have presented in the previous studies different interpretations that could account for the differential modulation observed for social and non-social uncertainty. Here we will discuss it in relation to the mounting experimental evidence on the role of feedback signals in primary visual area V1 (Petro et al. 2014).

7.4 Discussion

In this study we investigated whether activity in human primary visual areas reflected social and non-social reward and risk prediction errors (RePE and RiPE). We employed a trust game (social) and a card game (non-social), each made up of two distinct phases: outcome anticipation and outcome delivery. Throughout these two phases we manipulated degrees of social and non-social uncertainty along a comparable scale. In previous studies we showed how this manipulation allowed us to uncover a network of regions, including cortical and subcortical areas, reflecting both social and non-social prediction errors (Fig. 5.3; Fig. 6.3). Importantly, a functional connectivity analysis indicated that a region of the cuneus was influenced by the activity of the dorsal anterior cingulate cortex (dACC) coding for social and non-social prediction errors during outcome anticipation (Fig. 5.6).

First, to locate primary visual area V1 of each participant, we run a retinotopic mapping experiment. Then we run parametric analyses to test whether V1 activity reflected expected reward and risk modulations during outcome anticipation and delivery. Results from this set of analyses indicated that the combined activity of our participants' V1 areas reflected modulation of social and non-social uncertainty (RePE) during outcome anticipation (Fig. 7.3).

We also searched for subregions within the defined V1 areas responding to the same modulation found previously in dACC. Indeed as predicted by a functional connectivity analysis, we found that activity in a cluster of the cuneus reflected a non-social RiPE signal for card game trials and a social RePE signal for trust game trials (Fig. 7.4).

7.4.1 Overall and local activity in V1 and early visual areas reflects motivational prediction errors during anticipation of outcomes

In general two main classes of prediction errors have been reported in the literature. Perceptual prediction errors signal the degree of surprise with respect to a particular outcome. Motivational prediction errors report also the valence (sign) of the discrepancy between prediction and current state - not only whether the outcome was surprising, but also whether it was better or worse than expected. In most part perceptual prediction errors have been observed in cortical regions, whereas signed reward and punishment prediction errors have

151

generally been found in subcortical areas (den Ouden et al. 2012). However, subcortical unsigned prediction errors have also been observed in the primate midbrain (Matsumoto & Hikosaka 2009), human striatum (Zink et al. 2003; den Ouden et al. 2010), and in the ventral tegmental area (Bunzeck & Düzel 2006). Similarly though rarer, signed motivational error signals have also been reported in cortical areas, including the orbitofrontal cortex (Takahashi et al. 2009; O'Neill & Schultz 2010; O'Neill & Schultz 2013), the insular cortex (Pessiglione et al. 2006; Preuschoff et al. 2008), and in the medial prefrontal cortex (Matsumoto & Hikosaka 2007).

Our results are consistent with these latter findings indicating that even early visual area V1 activity might indeed reflect motivational prediction errors. Crucially our data show that this activity is not limited to the pure risk non-social domain and that it also correlates with varying degrees of social uncertainty.

As noted previously, two important features of a stimulus representing a decision alternative are its value and associated probability and their product formally predict optimal decision making (Von Neumann & Morgenstern 1944). Consequently one can vary the degree of value or probability and measure whether the different brain activation patterns reflect different computations. Although V1 was not traditionally thought to play a role in reward processing, recently a number of studies indicated that activity in V1 is modulated by manipulation of reward. Notably, V1 neurons in the rat have been shown to signal value (Shuler & Bear 2006), and a similar observation has been made in the macaque V1 (Stănişor et al. 2013). Other studies showed that value also influences activation levels within human early visual cortex, including V1 area, even in the absence of saccadic responses (Serences 2008; Serences & Saproo 2010). Our approach is complementary to the one used in these studies and focused on the other important feature of decisions alternatives, namely its reward probability. We studied modulations due to reward uncertainty during outcome anticipation and at outcome delivery, and found that overall V1 activity reflected a RePE signal during outcome anticipation (Fig. 7.3). Although we did not find correlation of the BOLD signal with outcome prediction errors, our data is consistent with a number of studies relating V1 activity with anticipation. In fact, anticipatory activity in V1 may in some instances be driven by dopaminergic input directly from the ventral tegmental area (Tan 2009) or indirectly from the prefrontal cortex (Noudoost & Moore 2011). This latter finding is all the more interesting as we found in a previous functional connectivity analysis that a region of the prefrontal cortex (dACC) influenced a cluster in the cuneus during outcome anticipation. Here we presented results indicating that indeed at a local level activity in early visual cortex reflected anticipation of outcomes in the form of a RiPE signal for non-social and RePE signal for social manipulations of uncertainty (Fig. 7.4).

One important question that arises from these results is related to the contribution of feedforward and feedback signals in generating reward value and reward uncertainty activity in V1. For instance, anticipatory haemodynamic signals in V1 have been found even without feedforward stimulation (Sirotin & Das 2009).

Today we know much of how V1 neurons respond to their selective stimulus, their cortical architecture and functional maps of columnar orientation preference and ocular dominance. Nonetheless most of these findings are related to the feedforward cascade of processing, mostly based on neuronal spiking as recorded in electrophysiology. However, recent studies show how this feedforward model can be updated to integrate the wealth of response properties brought back into V1 by cortical feedback (Petro et al. 2014; Muckli & Petro 2013). One technique that might be employed to rule out the influence of direct feedforward stimulation in the coding of reward uncertainty and value, consists in sampling feedback signals in non stimulated regions of V1 (Smith & Muckli 2010). This is possible because area V1 receives bottom-up (geniculate) and lateral (cortico-cortical) input from a small part of the visual field, and feedback from higher cortical areas from a larger part of the visual field. Such configuration allows to tease apart responses outside the classical receptive field, unrelated to bottom-up and lateral input, and instead related to cortical feedback. To do so one would need an experimental design that selectively eliminates feedforward input (by occluding part of the visual field and then mapping that into V1 areas) and investigate the activity in these non-feedforward stimulated areas. If modulation of the signal reflecting reward uncertainty in such defined non-stimulated areas survives then it can be ascribed to the influence of cortical feedback.

Finally, the account painted thus far is consistent with the mechanisms proposed by predictive coding theories (Friston 2005; Clark 2013), in which descending predictions originated in deep pyramidal cells are compared to the sensory signals received at lower levels of the hierarchy. Here the discrepancy between predictions and actual sensory data is computed and a prediction error arises. Then this information is transferred in the feedforward stream of the superficial pyramidal cells up to the next higher cortical level to update further the internal models. Further evidence is needed though to assess whether motivational prediction errors are indeed fed back to early visual areas, what function do they serve and what mechanism is used to update prediction and prediction error units - as suggested by predictive coding accounts (den Ouden et al. 2012).

7.4.2 Conclusion

In the two previous studies presented, we compared modulations due to social and non-social forms of uncertainty and showed that besides evidence in favour of a common currency theory (Ruff & Fehr 2014), the data also provides elements of divergence from such a model. In this study we replicated similar findings in early visual area V1. We found that overall activity in V1 reflected a RePE signal for both social and non-social modulations of reward uncertainty during outcome anticipation. This result represents an element of convergence to the idea that a common neural scale is employed in the processing of social and non-social types of rewards. Besides this observation we also found at a local level, as predicted by a previous connectivity analysis, a region responding differentially to social (RePE) and non-social (RiPE) manipulations of uncertainty during outcome anticipation.

Taken together these results are consistent with our previous findings and suggest that the type of feedback received and processed in early visual areas might include motivational prediction errors. Further experimentation, including designs that selectively investigate non-feedforward stimulated areas are needed.

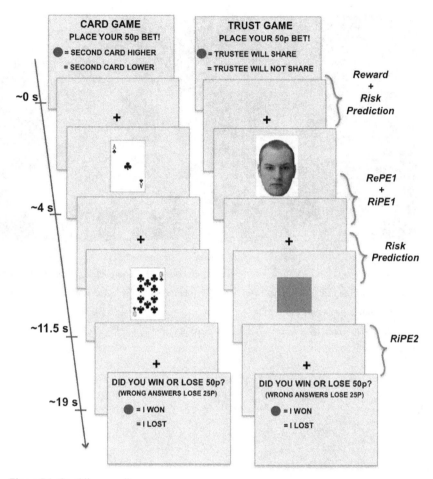

Figure 7.1. Gambling paradigm.

Participants played card game (CG) and trust game (TG) trials presented in random order. In card game trials they first bet on the second card presented being higher or lower than the first one. In trust game trials they bet on whether the trustee associated to that game was going to return a share or not. The timeline of the two types of gamble is identical. After placing their bet participants watch the first card or trustee's face followed 7.5s later by a second card or a coloured square (green=trustee shared; red=trustee kept). Finally participants were asked to confirm if they won or lost on that gamble. With display of the first card or trustee's face the initial constant reward and risk prediction is only partially resolved and a reward and risk prediction error occurs.

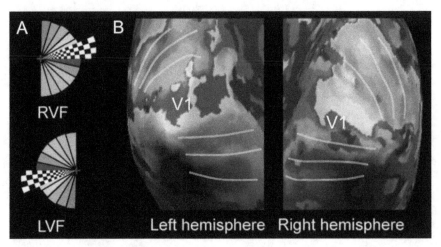

Fig. 7.2. Retinotopic mapping of early visual area V1.

Figures on the left (A) show a representation of the standard phase-encoded rotating checkerboard (stimulation) used in the experiment (RVF and LVF being right and left visual fields). Colour coded wedge-orientations (A) map to specific parts of primary visual cortex (B). Lines on the inflated cortex reconstruction (B) represent borders between early visual areas (only V1 is shown as this is the region of interest).

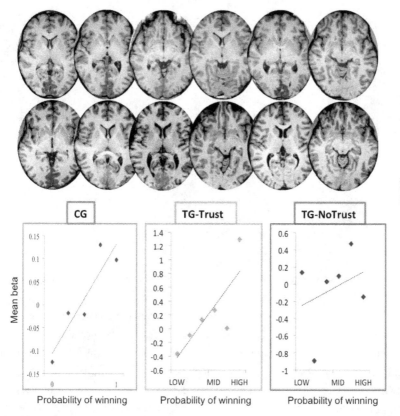

Figure 7.3. Early activity in V1 during outcome anticipation reflects modulation of social and non-social uncertainty.

Figures show an axial view of the 12 different brains scanned during the retinotopic experiment. Coloured ROIs represent the 12 V1 areas obtained. Plots show that activity within V1 areas (averaged across participants) to card game trials (CG) correlates positively with reward prediction error (RePE1) after first card. This first prediction error update is represented as a linear function of 5 reward probability conditions (x-axis represents probability of winning; see also Methods). Similarly activation in the same regions to both trust game subgroups of trials (TG-Trust and TG-NoTrust) correlates positively with a linear function of reward probability conditions as of display of trustee face (x-axis, from left to right, represents ascending reward probability conditions).

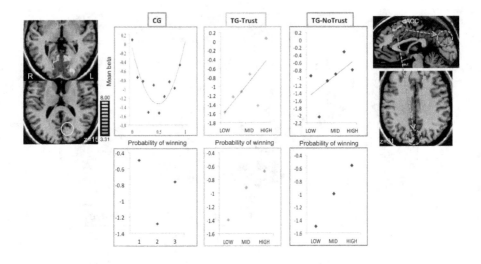

Figure 7.4. Early activity in a cluster of the cuneus during outcome anticipation reflects differential modulation of social and non-social uncertainty.

Figure in top left corner shows the combined volumes of interest (VOI) after overlapping V1 areas of 12 participants. Figure in bottom left corner (axial view) shows a statistical parametric map of the fixed effect analysis colour coded for the t-values (p<0.001 uncorrected, df=11). Figure in top right corner (sagittal view) shows the results of a functional connectivity analysis indicating that during outcome anticipation activity in the reference region dorsal anterior cingulate cortex (dACC in yellow) influences activity in a cluster of the cuneus (dark blue). Figure in bottom right corner (axial view) shows that this cluster partially overlaps with the combined V1-VOI mask (light blue).

Plots show that similarly to what found in dACC, neural activation in a cluster of the cuneus (x=-12; y=-72; z=22; 250 voxels; max stat=5.02) to card game trials (CG) correlates positively with risk prediction error after first card. This first prediction error update is represented as a U-shaped function of 10 reward probability conditions (top plot; x-axis represents probability of winning; dotted line best quadratic fit; see also Methods). Activation in the same cluster to both trust game subgroups of trials (TG-Trust and TG-NoTrust) correlates positively with a linear function of reward probability conditions as of display of trustee's face (top plots; x-axis, from left to right, represents ascending reward probability conditions; dotted lines best linear fit). Bottom plots represent the same type of effect by averaging CG and TG conditions in 3 bins representing 3 ascending levels of reward probability (see also Methods).

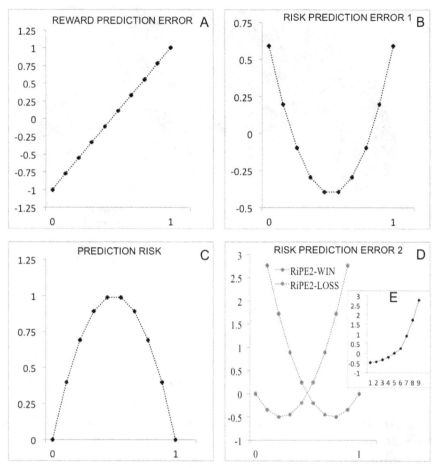

Figure 7.1S. Decision parameters functions.

Plots illustrate reward prediction error, risk prediction error and prediction risk as a function of the probability of winning after display of Card 1. Before Card 1 (or trustee's face) is revealed reward prediction error and prediction risk are constant. After Card 1 is revealed the error becomes a function of the probability of winning. The reward prediction error (A) is linear and the first risk prediction error (B) is quadratic (U-shaped) in the probability of winning. Before Card 2 is revealed, the risk prediction (C) is quadratic (inversely U-shaped). At outcome after Card 2 is revealed the error becomes a function of both the probability of winning at Card 1 and the actual win or loss. Therefore the second risk prediction error update (D) is represented by two symmetric functions that can be summarised in one single function (E) with nine values each representing one risk prediction error level for wins and the corresponding one for losses (more details can be found in Appendix I).

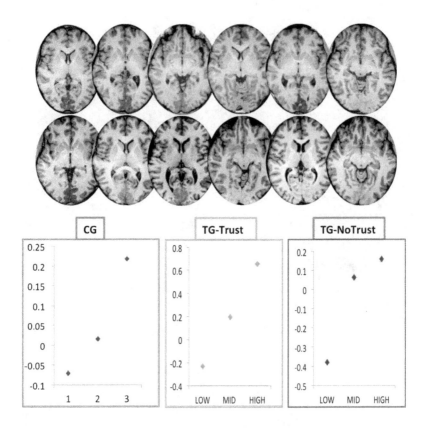

Figure 7.2S. Early activity in V1 during outcome anticipation reflects modulation of social and non-social uncertainty.

Figures show an axial view of the 12 different brains scanned during the retinotopic experiment. Coloured ROIs represent the 12 V1 areas obtained. Plots show that activity within V1 areas (averaged across participants) to card game trials (CG) correlates positively with reward prediction error (RePE1) after first card. This first prediction error update is represented as a linear function of the 3 averaged reward probability conditions (x-axis represents increasing probability of winning; see also Methods). Similarly activation in the same regions to both trust game subgroups of trials (TG-Trust and TG-NoTrust) correlates positively with a linear function of reward probability conditions as of display of trustee face (x-axis, from left to right, represents ascending reward probability conditions).

Table 7.1. Card game and trust game decision parameters values.

Reward probability at Card 1 (p)	RePE1	RiPE1	PR	RiPE2-Win	RiPE2-Loss
0*	-1	0.59	0		0
0.11*	-0.78	0.20	0.40	2.76	-0.34
0.22	-0.56	-0.10	0.69	1.73	-0.49
0.33	-0.33	-0.30	0.89	0.89	-0.44
0.44**	-0.11	-0.40	0.99	0.25	-0.20
0.56**	0.11	-0.40	0.99	-0.20	0.25
0.67	0.33	-0.30	0.89	-0.44	0.89
0.78	0.56	-0.10	0.69	-0.49	1.73
0.89***	0.78	0.20	0.40	-0.34	2.76
1***	1	0.59	0	0	

The table shows all decision parameter values for reward prediction error (RePE1), prediction risk (PR), risk prediction error at Card 1 (RiPE1) and at Card 2 (RiPE2-Win and RiPE2-Loss) corresponding to each initial reward probability condition at Card 1 (more details can be found in Appendix I).

*Corresponding values for low reward probability in trust game trials.

**Corresponding values for mid reward probability in trust game trials.

***Corresponding values for high reward probability in trust game trials.

III General Discussion and Future Directions

8 General Discussion

In the context of the current debate over the common or distinct neural basis of social and non-social forms of decision making, four of the results presented in this thesis are of particular interest: (a) largely similar subcortical networks are correlated with processing of social and non-social RePE during anticipation of outcomes; (b) activity in cortical regions reflects RiPE for non-social and RePE for social outcome anticipation; (c) cortical regions reflecting non-social RiPE at outcome delivery, also represent fairness and uncertainty but not monetary utility in a social setting; (d) activity in early visual areas reflect motivational prediction errors in both social and non-social settings.

Here we will further integrate these findings in light of current and past literature, discuss outstanding questions and indicate future directions of investigation.

8.1 Integrative view of findings

We have studied the neural representations of social and non-social forms of uncertainty using behavioural and neuroimaging techniques (fMRI) in humans. We used an experimental paradigm that makes direct comparisons of social and non-social representations possible. In fact, our paradigm differed from previous studies comparing social and non-social decision making in that, while keeping value constant, focused on varying comparable degrees of social and non-social uncertainty. To achieve this we used a card game paradigm (Preuschoff et al. 2006) that, in the absence of learning and salience confounds, could capture reward and risk predictions and subsequent errors in the non-social domain. We then designed a social trust game that maintained the same structure of the card game so that it could generate comparable social reward and risk predictions and errors. Importantly, besides manipulating degrees of social uncertainty our trust game could measure fairness of outcomes and the effects of gains and losses (monetary utility).

On the one hand this design had the advantage to expose the distributed network of regions responding to social and non-social RePE and RiPE. On the other hand it allowed to directly test how specific regions known to code for non-social RePE and RiPE respond to comparable changes in the social domain.

While the results of the studies reported do not support unilaterally the extended common currency or the social valuation specific schema (Ruff & Fehr 2014), they relate to them in several meaningful ways. Our results also add evidence to a recent model of the insular cortex as the centre of integration of uncertainty with bodily, affective and sensory information (Singer et al. 2009). Finally results provide initial evidence of motivational prediction errors in V1, adding to the bulk of recent research implicating this traditionally only-visual region with a variety of higher cortical feedback signals (Petro et al. 2014). We have seen earlier how predictive coding accounts (Clark 2013) initially applied to the physiology of early visual areas (and in particular V1), have been recently used to model the working of regions involved with processing reward and emotions (Seth 2013). The flexibility of this general model of brain function is such that one can hypothesise that processes traditionally thought to be typical of one region, actually are used in other systems carrying different functions. In our third study, using this logic we set up to look for motivational prediction and prediction error signals in primary visual areas generally thought to encode only perceptual prediction errors. Our results indeed provided some initial evidence in favour of this flexibility of the general predictive coding model, and showed that the overall activity of functionally derived V1 areas correlated with RePE.

8.1.1 Interpreting the cortical-subcortical divide during outcome anticipation

The results of the first study presented expose a divide between subcortical and cortical regions when comparing the way these regions process social and non-social forms of uncertainty. In fact we found that activity in subcortical regions such as the ventral striatum during outcome anticipation reflected RePE in both social and non-social domains. On the contrary, activity in cortical regions such as anterior insula and dACC during outcome anticipation did not reflect a similar neural response profile in both domains. Activity in these regions correlated with RiPE in the non-social domain and with RePE in the social domain (Fig. 5.3, 5.4, 5.5).

It is important to note that the correlative nature of these results makes the task of assigning a conclusive interpretation to these observations difficult. In fact, if we consider the case when subcortical regions (Fig. 5.4) reflect social and non-social uncertainty, this result speaks in favour of the extended common currency schema but it is still possible to think of alternative interpretations. For instance standard (3T) fMRI measurements might not provide enough spatial resolution to resolve whether different types of uncertainty recruit distinct neural populations in a given brain area.

Indeed, the competing theory proposes that within these regions there might be separation of specific neural populations coding for social and non-social aspects of the world. In support of this hypothesis, studies using single neuron recording in non-human primates have started to identify different types of neurons in the striatum selectively encoding social versus non-social aspects of rewards. In one study neurons in the striatum have been found to respond to social (images of conspecifics) or non-social (juice) rewards (Klein et al. 2013). Another study identified neurons of the striatum involved in signalling either when a reward was given or when this reward was due to the action of the monkey or a conspecific (Baez-Mendoza et al. 2013). In addition, some pharmacological studies indicate differentiation in the neuronal basis of social and non-social value coding. In one study, the effects of oxytocin on social behaviour revealed neural modulations in value-related regions without concomitant dopamine release (Striepens et al. 2014). This is all the more interesting when considering that BOLD responses in these same regions for non-social decisions are affected by pharmacological modulation of the dopamine system (Pessiglione et al. 2006). Therefore it might be the case that social and non-social decision making actually rely on parallel neural computations that follow similar principles (for instance coding of RePE in ventral striatum) but that are nevertheless localised in overlapping neural circuits specialised for processing one type of information (in accordance with the social-valuation-specific schema). Besides single neuron studies that can only be performed in humans for clinical purposes, evidence for such distinct neural populations could also be obtained using methods such as high-resolution fMRI (Harel 2012), repetition suppression paradigms where the same stimulus elicits reduced activity in neurons specialised for this stimulus (Grill-spector et al. 2006) or methods such as multivariate pattern analyses (Haxby 2012) in conjunction with specifically designed paradigms.

Likewise, the results found in cortical regions (Fig. 5.3) reflecting RiPE in the non-social domain and RePE in the social domain, speak in favour of the social-valuation-specific schema. Nonetheless even in this circumstance it is possible to put forward alternative interpretations. In fact, as the extended version of the common currency schema suggests, the differential activation might be due to the influence of other separate anatomical regions specifically involved when social or non-social factors are at play. In other words, even shared neural processes in some regions may still depend on interactions with distinct brain networks that encode either social or non-social aspects of the environment. In this case, the main difference in neural processing during social and non-social decisions might be due not to local value computations but rather to the influence of remote neural regions that provide the information on which these different computations are based. Supporting this view, a number of studies investigating social decisions report responses correlated with the construction of uniquely social values in regions outside the classic reward circuitry such as the dlPFC (Baumgartner et al. 2011), temporo parietal junction (Carter et al. 2012) and dmPFC (Nicolle et al. 2012). In this context is of particular importance to develop connectivity analyses that can help disentangle these questions. For instance a number of studies have revealed that different types of social decision making and learning involve functional coupling between BOLD responses in regions known to process value and BOLD responses in regions outside the reward circuitry (Behrens et al. 2008; Baumgartner et al. 2011). Generally though, one crucial problem is that these effects in social contexts remain to be established by direct comparisons of how social versus non-social decisions might change patterns of connectivity.

In our first study we start to address this problem using a combination of functional connectivity analyses (Granger Causality Mapping or GCM, and Psychophysiological Interaction or PPI; Fig. 5.6, 5.7; Table 5.4) comparing a more correlational type of connectivity (PPI) with the direction of influence of the identified regions of interest (GCM) while processing social and non-social factors (a simplified model of these results is presented here in Fig. 8.1). The overall picture shows that in the non-social domain cortical regions seem to influence and being influenced by subcortical regions to a much lesser extent compared to the social domain. This observation is reflected in the different response profiles found for social and non-social outcome anticipation (Fig. 8.1, 5.3 and 5.4). On the one hand when the response profile for outcome anticipation (RePE) is the same for subcortical and cortical regions (social domain), this is reflected in a higher frequency of functional connectivity between these two groups of regions. On the other hand, when the response profile for outcome anticipation is distinct (non-social domain) for subcortical (RePE) and cortical regions (RiPE), this instead is reflected in a lower level of influence between subcortical and cortical regions. In this context it is particularly interesting the functional connection, observed only in the social domain, between bilateral ventral striatum and regions of the mPFC (including dmPFC previously implicated in the construction of uniquely social values; Nicolle et al. 2012). It is also interesting to note the bidirectional influence, observed only in the social domain, between bilateral ventral striatum and OFC. This observation might be related to the fact that OFC is thought to be critical in motivational decision making only when this requires a model-based value computation (Stalnaker et al. 2015). In other words, when the behaviour is based on previous experience, which would allow a relevant value to be pre-computed without simulating the future and without integrating new information, then OFC is not necessary. However, when a novel value needs to be computed on the fly using new information or predictions that have been acquired since the original learning, then OFC is required. One could then reason that in the context of non-social pure risk where outcome distributions are known (and explicit), OFC engages mainly other cortical structures and sends neural information rather than receiving. Differently, in the context of social decision making where outcome distributions are not explicitly accessible and new information needs to be integrated (e.g. emotional value of social stimuli), OFC would engage also subcortical structures and overall receive neural information rather than sending.

Finally, though we did not find significant functional connectivity in the GCM with amygdala during outcome anticipation, the PPI analysis revealed connectivity between the left anterior insula cluster and bilateral amygdala (Table 5.4). This was in addition to the results from the parametric analysis revealing that only left amygdala was specifically involved in processing social prediction errors (Fig. 5.5). This structure is well known as a region responsible for emotional processing and is thought to be critical to social behaviour (Adolphs 2009). It is therefore plausible to think that amygdala would act as the subcortical counterpart of those cortical regions implicated with the construction of uniquely social values outside the classic reward circuitry (dlPFC, temporo parietal junction, dmPFC; see studies mentioned above).

8.1.2 Integration of RiPE, fairness and monetary utility

The results from the second study integrate the concept of RiPE in a non-social setting with that of fairness and its relation to monetary utility maximisation in a social setting. We found that among other cortical regions (dACC and OFC), and as predicted by previous models (Singer et al. 2009; Seth 2013), anterior insula's activity represented a similar integration of social and non-social uncertainty. In particular activity reflected modulation of non-social RiPE as well as fairness and level of reward uncertainty of social outcomes (Fig. 6.3, 6.4).

On a different note, we discussed earlier the results of studies showing processing of fairness in insula using the ultimatum game (Sanfey et al. 2003, 2007; Tabibnia et al. 2008). Importantly these results do not confirm that the insula is responding to unfairness as it could simply be encoding a negative prediction error representing the player's own payoff. To tease apart this alternative explanation, we used a trust game where fairness and own-payoff could vary independently. This allowed on the one hand to test for fairness effects in the same regions coding for non-social RiPE (as discussed above), and on the other hand to test whether this effect was only a reflection of own payoff. Results showed that anterior insula activation (together with dACC and OFC) is indeed correlated to fairness of outcome independently of own payoff (Fig. 6.3, 6.5).

Also, it is generally thought that the anterior insula detects actual and potential deviations from socially acceptable outcomes (fairness of outcomes) and thus provides the information necessary to guide choices towards rectifying these deviations. Our results support this idea as they show that anterior insula is modulated by the fairness of outcomes as well as the degree of uncertainty. At the same time our results raise the question of how this region can compute fairness. In fact we showed that while anterior insula signalled fairness and uncertainty of outcomes, it did not reflect monetary utility (Fig. 6.3, 6.5). Given that in order to compute fairness it is necessary to compare potential gains and losses against the actual social outcome, it seems plausible to postulate that in a social context such computations require the intervention of other regions (for instance dlPFC), compared with the non-social situation (where RiPE does reflect monetary utility). Supporting this view, Baumgartner and colleagues (2011) using the ultimatum game, and combining both causal (TMS) and imaging (fMRI) techniques, found that although the stimulation of right dlPFC caused a large reduction in the rejection rate of unfair offers, the anterior insula was equally activated across treatments. These findings also suggest that insula's activity reflects that of an "unfairness detector" as it is not directly involved in the rectification of unfairness.

8.1.3 A speculative integration of the common currency and social valuation-specific schemas

In light of the observations put forward so far we propose an integration of the different models discussed. Our data suggest that both the extended common currency and the social valuation specific schemas might both be operating in the human brain. It is helpful to use the anterior insula, one of the key regions studied, as a reference model for such integration.

In the model proposed by Singer and colleagues (2009) anterior insula is thought to be the centre of integration between subcortical and higher cortical regions. Here predictive feeling states are compared with current feeling states and give rise to feeling state prediction errors. Such a model is closely related to the general structure assumed by predictive coding accounts (Clark 2013), even though here the notion of prediction error is expressed in terms of change detection and salience rather than through mechanisms of predictive coding. In this model the insular cortex would integrate external sensory and internal physiological signals with computations about their uncertainty. The product of this integration is then thought to modulate social and motivational decision making in conjunction with bodily homeostasis (Fig. 8.2).

In a closely related model of interoceptive inference (Seth 2013) the anterior insular cortex is depicted as a comparator key region within the extended autonomic neural substrate. Using the framework of predictive coding, this model proposes that emotional content (e.g. response to unfairness) is generated by top-down inference of the causes of interoceptive signals. So anterior insula would both compare top-down predictions against bottom-up prediction errors, and be a source of anticipatory visceromotor control. Overall this model extends two main functions of insular cortex as supporting error-based learning of feeling states and uncertainty (Singer et al. 2009) and as responding to interoceptive mismatches that for instance underlie anxiety (Paulus & Stein 2006).

On one hand results provide experimental evidence that expands on the predictions postulated by the above models of anterior insula. On the other hand they speak to the more general problem of how social and non-social information could actually be integrated in the human brain.

Consider from a more integrated perspective what the results observed in anterior insula during the anticipation and outcome phase could add to these models. In one case we have the situation where activity in anterior insula seems to be encoding mainly reward anticipation in a quantitative manner (Fig. 5.3), while at the same time it appears to not account for the social dimension of trustworthiness per se. In this case anterior insula seems to give way to the more financial quantitative dimension of reward expectation over the more socially relevant dimension of trust. In the other case we have a situation opposite to what observed previously, showing that the picture described above can be inverted. In fact in this case activation in anterior insula (Fig. 6.3) seems to encode mainly fairness of outcomes but not the more quantitative reward dimension. So it appears that now anterior insula seems to give way to the more socially relevant dimension of fairness over the more quantitative dimension of financial reward. Nonetheless even in this case anterior insula showcases the ability to encode a more quantitative general uncertainty dimension embedded in the game (Fig. 6.4, modulation due to high outcome prediction error).

One could reason that anterior insula not only integrates information coming from different modality-specific feeling states but also could give way to one type depending on connectivity or other factors. For instance, the type of connectivity we observed during outcome anticipation where anterior insula engages the frontal and subcortical regions while it is engaged by dACC and ventral striatum (Fig. 8.1) could represent a specific scenario of integrative activity where a more quantitative (value-based-like) channel is employed. It follows the prediction of a substantially different connectivity picture at the outcome stage where instead a more social-value-specific channel might be privileged. In this case it is plausible to hypothesise the key contribution of social-specific regions such as the dmPFC, dlPFC and the temporal parietal junction (Baumgartner et al. 2011; Carter et al. 2012; Nicolle et al. 2012).

Now with respect to the model of anterior insula proposed by Singer et al. (2009), our results seem to support two of the four key mechanisms postulated, namely, the dimension of a specific feeling state and the parallel mechanism that deals with uncertainty (besides contextual appraisal and individual preferences that were not measured in our studies; Fig. 8.2). In light of what we observed above we could add a new label to this schema indicating that the interaction of the four mechanisms might depend on a more general supervising mechanism that might privilege one modality over another depending on context (e.g. socially relevant or not). For instance in the context of our strategic social game the system might have privileged tracking of reward prediction over other parallel feeling states during the anticipation phase. Differently, once the game was over the system might have privileged tracking of relevant social types of valuation over the more quantitative aspect of reward processing.

A similar mechanism would also provide a model of how the common currency and social-valuation specific schemas could work side by side. In fact depending on context the system could engage a more general value representation circuit, leading the experimenter to label such configuration as common currency schema. In our study this is more likely to be associated to the anticipation of outcome phase. Whether in a different context the same system could engage a more specific social value circuit, leading the experiment to label such configuration as social valuation-specific schema. In our study this is more likely to be associated with the events observed at outcome delivery. Therefore both schemas might be operating under the supervision of the same general mechanism hypothesised before.

It is important to observe that our interpretation of the data might be incomplete and that some crucial aspect of the social and non-social neural integration might not be picked up by our experimental design. In fact an alternative dynamic to the one depicted above is plausible. This is because in the context of our trust games the two dimensions representing reward processing and social valuation of trust or fairness might actually be processed simultaneously in anterior insula. One reason why we did not observe an interaction between the two dimensions could be related to the fact that participants chose less frequently the TG-NoTrust condition (low power). This is an aspect worth exploring in future experimentation using a different design. In particular it would be crucial to find clever paradigms that could separate the two dimensions (so that they would become orthogonal) hypothesised to be processed in parallel in the context of the same strategic game.

8.2 Outstanding Questions and Future Directions

We discussed earlier that monetary utility maximisation can conflict with fairness maximisation, and this behavioural observation is reflected in the neural activity of key regions such as anterior insula and dlPFC. These observations raise the question of how the brain actually attaches value to money and brings to question what is the evolutionary origin of the mechanism that values money. Understanding the natural object that our monetary systems evolved to value might explain some of the inconsistencies we observe when humans place subjective values on money (Glimcher 2011). The results presented here as well as many other studies point to the possibility that money attaches itself to the neural mechanisms that evolved for placing values on social interactions. Currently these neural mechanisms and their underlying algorithmic structure remain elusive.

One other general question arising when comparing different forms of uncertainty is whether and how actual probability is represented. We know that this quantity is associated with the neurotransmitter dopamine and with reinforcement learning. But this mechanism does not represent probabilities explicitly, as it merges probability and value together. At the same time behavioural studies show how explicitly encoded probabilities influence choice in inconsistent ways (Kahneman & Tversky 1979). The question then arises of whether and how in the brain are encoded explicit probabilities as a separable quantity from utilities or subjective values.

This last open question is related to the way we can think of different forms of uncertainty as a continuum between known and unknown distribution of outcomes. In such continuum probabilities can be known (pure risk), partially known (ambiguity) or unknown (social ambiguity). Further experimentation is needed in order to provide a mechanistic account and spatiotemporal characterisation of the "choice" and "outcome" stages of decision making in the human brain under these different forms of social and non-social uncertainty.

In earlier sections we said that the choice phase is critical for understanding how decision makers perceive and integrate information under different forms of uncertainty. Sequential sampling models of binary decision-making have been used extensively to provide a mechanistic account of perceptual decisions (Ratcliff & McKoon 2008; Philiastides & Sajda 2006) and more recently value and preference-based choices (Krajbich et al. 2010; Krajbich & Rangel 2011). These models posit that decisions involve an integrative mechanism in which the relative sensory or value signals supporting different decision alternatives accumulate over time to an internal decision boundary (Ratcliff 1978). The drift diffusion model is one example of such sequential sampling models. This model decomposes behavioural data (accuracy and response times) into internal components of processing, thereby providing a mechanistic account of the underlying decision process. Future work could make use of this model to compare the decision process in different economic games designed to represent distinct forms of uncertainty and provide mechanistic insights into the differences across these games. For instance games could comprise a two-alternative forced choice task (reaction time task) between a sure but small payoff (keep option) and an uncertain high-payoff (play option) for which the nature of uncertainty will depend on the game. One possibility is to design non-social gambling games where uncertainty can take the form of an explicit reward/win probability (pure risk) or a range of possible probabilities (pure ambiguity). These could then be compared with a social game (similar to our trust game), where uncertain high-payoff will depend on a more or less trustworthy partner's strategy (social ambiguity). A mechanistic account of the behavioural changes across the three uncertainty conditions could then be provided by fitting the drift diffusion model to the behavioural data to generate predictions relating to changes in internal components of processing.

Another possible future direction stemming from the current work could focus on the outcome phase of decision making. We saw earlier how using the appropriate paradigms, during the outcome phase two types of neural signals, namely the reward prediction error (RePE) and risk prediction error (RiPE), are updated every time decision makers receive novel information related to anticipated and actual rewards. To date, the full spatiotemporal dynamics of RePE and RiPE and how these signals vary across different source of decision uncertainty remain unknown. A similar paradigm employed here (Preuschoff et al. 2006) and adapted to studying pure risk, pure ambiguity and social ambiguity, could be employed in conjunction with multimodal neuroimaging (EEG/fMRI).

For instance trial-by-trial variability in temporally specific EEG components could be used to build parametric BOLD predictors for RePE and RiPE and identify the generators of these signals. This analysis framework could be applied to each of the three different forms of uncertainty (pure risk, pure ambiguity and social ambiguity) to study the extent to which these share the same computational principles and neural representations.

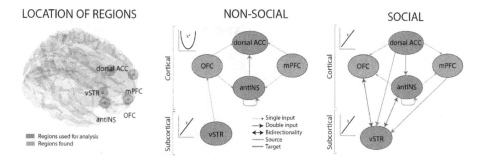

LOCATION OF REGIONS   NON-SOCIAL   SOCIAL

Figure 8.1. Simplified model of functional connectivity (GCM) and response profile for social and non-social outcome anticipation (see also Fig. 5.6 and 5.7).

Blue and green arrows indicate the direction of influence between reference regions (in red) and source and target regions. In particular, blue indicates influence from a reference region to a target region. Green indicates influence from a source region to a reference region. The dark double arrow indicates both source and target influences. In both social and non-social domain, regions are grouped in cortical and subcortical. Each group is also paired with a response profile type (either linear or quadratic) as found in our analysis of outcome anticipation (Fig. 5.3 and 5.4). Overall the model shows differences in connectivity between the social and non-social domain. Not only functional connectivity differs in cortical regions but also between these and the subcortical regions. Regions abbreviations: antINS (anterior insula); dorsal ACC (dorsal anterior cingulate cortex); OFC (orbitofrontal cortex); mPFC (medial prefrontal cortex); vSTR (ventral striatum).

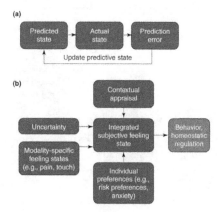

Figure 8.2. Model of the integration of feelings, empathy and uncertainty in insular cortex (from Singer et al. 2009).

(a) Schematic of error-based learning: a predicted state is followed by the actual (experienced) state. The difference between the two, the prediction error, is used to update the predicted state such that future predicted states will be more accurate. (b) The integrated subjective feeling state combines information about modality-specific feelings, uncertainty, contextual appraisal and individual preferences and traits such as risk preferences and anxiety.

Appendix

I - Illustration of decision parameters

(Adapted from Preuschoff et al. 2008)

If we look at the timeline of the task (Fig. 5.1) we see that before display of the first stimulus our task is to predict our expected reward. Before display of the second stimulus our task is to predict the actual outcome. After seeing the first and second stimulus our prediction is corrected and a prediction error signal generated.

We call PR1 (prediction risk) the expected size of the error generated after seeing the first stimulus, and PR2 the expected size of the error generated after seeing the second stimulus.
We call RiPE1 the error that arises as a result of seeing stimulus 1 (expected reward), and RiPE2 the error that arises as a result of seeing stimulus 2 (actual reward).

In order to calculate the above metrics of risk we need to work out first the reward prediction errors (RePE).
RePE1 is the combined expected value of winning and losing after stimulus 1, minus the expected value prediction - this is zero being the probability of winning or losing fixed at choice: p=0.5 => EV=(0.5)1+(0.5)(-1)=0. If the probability of winning after stimulus 1 is p=1/9 then:

$$\text{RePE1} = \left[(1)\left(\frac{1}{9}\right) + (-1)\left(\frac{8}{9}\right) \right] - 0 = -0.77$$

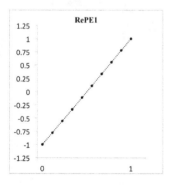

RePE2 is the difference of the actual outcome (1 or -1) and the previous RePE1. So in the case of a win is:

$$\mathrm{Re}\,PE2 = 1 - (-0.77) = 1.77$$

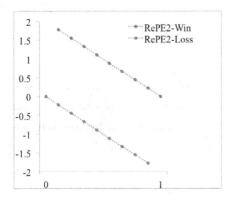

If we keep value fixed and we have 10 possible probabilities of winning as a result of display of stimulus 1 (p=0/9,1/9,2/9...9/9) the risk metrics are as follows.

PR1 is constant and is calculated as the expected size-squared of all possible reward prediction errors.

$$\mathrm{PR1} = \frac{1}{10}\left[2\left(\frac{1}{9}\right)^2 + 2\left(\frac{3}{9}\right)^2 + 2\left(\frac{5}{9}\right)^2 + 2\left(\frac{7}{9}\right)^2 + 2(1)^2\right] = 0.41$$

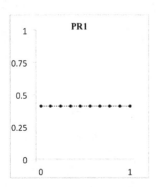

It then follows that RiPE1 changes as a function of the 10 probabilities of reward and is calculated as the difference between the squared reward prediction errors (RePE1) and PR1. For instance when the probability of winning after stimulus 1 is 1/9 then:

$$RiPE1 = (RePE1)^2 - PR1 = \left[(1)\left(\frac{1}{9}\right) + (-1)\left(\frac{8}{9}\right)\right]^2 - 0.41 = 0.20$$

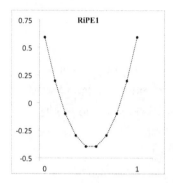

Next in the timeline we will have a second prediction risk signal (PR2) followed after the presentation of the outcome by a second risk prediction error (RiPE2).

In the mean-variance or risk-return financial model risk is defined as variance/standard deviation or second moment (see chapter 1).

PR2 this time changes as a function of the first reward prediction errors. This is calculated by taking the square of the RePE1 summed to the final reward value (1 or -1) and weighting them with the two respective probabilities (of winning or losing).

For instance when the probability of winning after stimulus 1 is 1/9 then:

$$PR2 = \frac{1}{9}[1 - (-0.77)]^2 + \frac{8}{9}[-1 - (-0.77)]^2 = 0.40$$

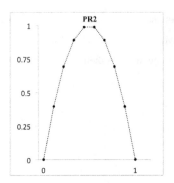

It then follows that RiPE2 changes as a function of the 10 probabilities of reward and the actual outcome. This is calculated as the difference between the respective squared reward prediction error (RePE2) and the prediction risk (PR2). If the probability of winning was 1/9 and the outcome was a win then:

$$\text{RiPE2} = (\text{RePE2})^2 - PR2 = (1.77)^2 - 0.40 = 2.74$$

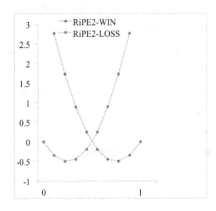

References

Adolphs, R. et al., 1995. Fear and the human amygdala. *The Journal of neuroscience : the official journal of the Society for Neuroscience*, 15(9), pp.5879–5891.

Adolphs, R., 2009. The social brain: neural basis of social knowledge. *Annual review of psychology*, 60, pp.693–716.

Adolphs, R., Tranel, D. & Damasio, A.R., 1998. The human amygdala in social judgment. *Nature*, 393(6684), pp.470–474.

Aharon, I. et al., 2001. Beautiful faces have variable reward value: fMRI and behavioral evidence. *Neuron*, 32(3), pp.537–51.

Alink, A. et al., 2010. Stimulus predictability reduces responses in primary visual cortex. *The Journal of neuroscience : the official journal of the Society for Neuroscience*, 30(8), pp.2960–2966.

Allman, J.M. et al., 2010. The von Economo neurons in frontoinsular and anterior cingulate cortex in great apes and humans. *Brain structure & function*, 214(5-6), pp.495–517.

Apicella, P. et al., 1991. Responses to reward in monkey dorsal and ventral striatum. *Experimental Brain Research*, 85(3).

Arnal, L.H. et al., 2009. Dual neural routing of visual facilitation in speech processing. *The Journal of neuroscience : the official journal of the Society for Neuroscience*, 29(43), pp.13445–13453.

Bach, D.R. et al., 2011. The known unknowns: neural representation of second-order uncertainty, and ambiguity. *The Journal of neuroscience : the official journal of the Society for Neuroscience*, 31(13), pp.4811–20.

Bach, D.R., Seymour, B. & Dolan, R.J., 2009. Neural activity associated with the passive prediction of ambiguity and risk for aversive events. *The Journal of neuroscience : the official journal of the Society for Neuroscience*, 29(6), pp.1648–56.

Báez-Mendoza, R., Harris, C.J. & Schultz, W., 2013. Activity of striatal neurons reflects social action and own reward. *Proceedings of the National Academy of Sciences of the United States of America*, 110(41), pp.16634–9.

Baumgartner, T. et al., 2011. Dorsolateral and ventromedial prefrontal cortex orchestrate normative choice. *Nature Neuroscience*, 14(11), pp.1468–1474.

Baxter, M.G. & Murray, E. a, 2002. The amygdala and reward. *Nature reviews. Neuroscience*, 3(7), pp.563–73.

Bechara, A. & Damasio, A.R., 2005. The somatic marker hypothesis: A neural theory of economic decision. *Games and Economic Behavior*, 52(2), pp.336–372.

Behrens, T.E.J. et al., 2008. Associative learning of social value. *Nature*, 456(7219), pp.245–9.

Belin, P. et al., 2000. Voice-selective areas in human auditory cortex. *Nature*, 403(6767), pp.309–12.

Berg, J., Dickhaut, J. & McCabe, K., 1995. Trust, Reciprocity, and Social History. *Games and Economic Behavior*, 10(1), pp.122–142.

Bernoulli, D., 1954. Exposition of a new theory on the measurement of risk. *Econometrica*, 22(1), pp.23–36.

Bossaerts, P., 2010. Risk and risk prediction error signals in anterior insula. *Brain structure & function*, 214(5-6), pp.645–53.

Bossaerts, P., 2009. What Decision Neuroscience Teaches Us About Financial Decision Making. *Annual Review of Financial Economics*, 1(1), pp.383–404.

Bray, S. & O'Doherty, J., 2007. Neural coding of reward-prediction error signals during classical conditioning with attractive faces. *Journal of neurophysiology*, 97(4), pp.3036–45.

Budd, J.M., 1998. Extrastriate feedback to primary visual cortex in primates: a quantitative analysis of connectivity. *Proceedings. Biological sciences / The Royal Society*, 265(1400), pp.1037–44.

Bunzeck, N. & Düzel, E., 2006. Absolute coding of stimulus novelty in the human substantia nigra/VTA. *Neuron*, 51(3), pp.369–79.

Bush, G. et al., 2002. Dorsal anterior cingulate cortex: a role in reward-based decision making. *Proceedings of the National Academy of Sciences of the United States of America*, 99(1), pp.523–8.

Bzdok, D. et al., 2011. ALE meta-analysis on facial judgments of trustworthiness and attractiveness. *Brain Structure and Function*, 215(3-4), pp.209–223.

Calder, A.J. et al., 2011. *The Oxford Handbook of Face Perception*, Oxford University Press.

Calder, A.J., Lawrence, A.D. & Young, A.W., 2001. Neuropsychology of fear and loathing. *Nature reviews. Neuroscience*, 2(5), pp.352–363.

Camerer, C., 2003. *Behavioral Game Theory: Experiments in Strategic Interaction*, Princeton University Press.

Camerer, C. & Weber, M., 1992. Recent developments in modeling preferences: Uncertainty and ambiguity. *Journal of Risk and Uncertainty*, 5(4), pp.325–370.

Caplin, A. & Dean, M., 2008. Dopamine, Reward Prediction Error, and Economics *.

Quarterly Journal of Economics, 123(2), pp.663–701.

Caplin, A. & Dean, M., 2007. The neuroeconomic theory of learning. In *American Economic Review*. pp. 148–152.

Carter, R.M. et al., 2012. A Distinct Role of the Temporal-Parietal Junction in Predicting Socially Guided Decisions. *Science*, 337(6090), pp.109–111.

Christopoulos, G.I. et al., 2009. Neural correlates of value, risk, and risk aversion contributing to decision making under risk. *The Journal of neuroscience : the official journal of the Society for Neuroscience*, 29(40), pp.12574–83.

Clark, A., 2013. Whatever next? Predictive brains, situated agents, and the future of cognitive science. *Behavioral and Brain Sciences*, 36(03), pp.181–204.

Cohen, J.Y. et al., 2012. Neuron-type-specific signals for reward and punishment in the ventral tegmental area. *Nature*, 482(7383), pp.85–8.

Coleman, J.S., 1990. Foundations of Social Theory. *Social Forces*, 69(2), p.993.

Cooper, J.C. et al., 2014. The role of the posterior temporal and medial prefrontal cortices in mediating learning from romantic interest and rejection. *Cerebral cortex (New York, N.Y. : 1991)*, 24(9), pp.2502–11.

Coricelli, G. & Nagel, R., 2009. Neural correlates of depth of strategic reasoning in medial prefrontal cortex. *Proceedings of the National Academy of Sciences*, 106(23), pp.9163–9168.

Coricelli, G. & Rustichini, A., 2010. Counterfactual thinking and emotions: regret and envy learning. *Philosophical transactions of the Royal Society of London. Series B, Biological sciences*, 365(1538), pp.241–7.

Craig, a D.B., 2009. How do you feel--now? The anterior insula and human awareness. *Nature reviews. Neuroscience*, 10(1), pp.59–70.

Critchley, H.D. & Rolls, E.T., 1996. Hunger and satiety modify the responses of olfactory and visual neurons in the primate orbitofrontal cortex. *Journal of neurophysiology*, 75(4), pp.1673–86.

d'Acremont, M. et al., 2009. Neural correlates of risk prediction error during reinforcement learning in humans. *NeuroImage*, 47(4), pp.1929–39.

Dalgleish, T., 2004. The emotional brain. *Nature reviews. Neuroscience*, 5(7), pp.583–589.

Damasio, A.R., 1994. *Descartes' Error: Emotion, Reason, and the Human Brain*, G.P. Putnam.

Daw, N.D. & Tobler, P.N., 2014. Chapter 15 - Value Learning through Reinforcement: The Basics of Dopamine and Reinforcement Learning. In P. W. G. B. T.-N. (Second E. Fehr, ed. San Diego: Academic Press, pp. 283–298.

Decety, J. et al., 2004. The neural bases of cooperation and competition: An fMRI investigation. *NeuroImage*, 23(2), pp.744–751.

Delgado, M.R., Frank, R.H. & Phelps, E.A., 2005. Perceptions of moral character modulate the neural systems of reward during the trust game. *Nature neuroscience*, 8(11), pp.1611–8.

Derbyshire, S.W.G. et al., 1997. Pain processing during three levels of noxious stimulation produces differential patterns of central activity. *Pain*, 73(3), pp.431–445.

Dreher, J.-C., Kohn, P. & Berman, K.F., 2006. Neural coding of distinct statistical properties of reward information in humans. *Cerebral cortex (New York, N.Y. : 1991)*, 16(4), pp.561–73.

Duerden, E.G. et al., 2013. Lateralization of affective processing in the insula. *NeuroImage*, 78, pp.159–75.

Eberhardt, J.L. et al., 2006. Looking deathworthy perceived stereotypicality of black defendants predicts capital-sentencing outcomes. *Psychological Science*, 17(5), pp.383–386.

Ellsberg, D., 1961. Risk, Ambiguity, and the Savage Axioms. *The Quarterly Journal of Economics*, 75(4), p.643.

Engell, A.D., Haxby, J. V & Todorov, A., 2007. Implicit trustworthiness decisions: automatic coding of face properties in the human amygdala. *Journal of cognitive neuroscience*, 19(9), pp.1508–19.

Fang, F., Kersten, D. & Murray, S.O., 2008. Perceptual grouping and inverse fMRI activity patterns in human visual cortex. *Journal of vision*, 8(7), pp.2.1–9.

Fecteau, S. et al., 2007. Diminishing risk-taking behavior by modulating activity in the prefrontal cortex: a direct current stimulation study. *The Journal of neuroscience : the official journal of the Society for Neuroscience*, 27(46), pp.12500–12505.

Fehr, E., Bernhard, H. & Rockenbach, B., 2008. Egalitarianism in young children. *Nature*, 454(7208), pp.1079–83.

Fehr, E. & Camerer, C.F., 2007. Social neuroeconomics: the neural circuitry of social preferences. *Trends in Cognitive Sciences*, 11(10), pp.419–427.

Fehr, E. & Krajbich, I., 2014. Chapter 11 - Social Preferences and the Brain. In P. W. G. B. T.-N. (Second E. Fehr, ed. San Diego: Academic Press, pp. 193–218.

Fibiger, H.C. & Phillips, A.G., 2011. Reward, Motivation, Cognition: Psychobiology of Mesotelencephalic Dopamine Systems. In R. Terjung, ed. *Comprehensive Physiology*.

Hoboken, NJ, USA: John Wiley & Sons, Inc.

Fiorillo, C.D., Tobler, P.N. & Schultz, W., 2003. Discrete coding of reward probability and uncertainty by dopamine neurons. *Science (New York, N.Y.)*, 299(5614), pp.1898–902.

Flowe, H.D. & Humphries, J.E., 2011. An examination of criminal face bias in a random sample of police lineups. *Applied Cognitive Psychology*, 25(2), pp.265–273.

Fouragnan, E. et al., 2013. The neurobiology of rewards and values in social decision making. *The Journal of neuroscience : the official journal of the Society for Neuroscience*, 33(8), pp.3602–11.

Friston, K., 2005. A theory of cortical responses. *Philosophical transactions of the Royal Society of London. Series B, Biological sciences*, 360(1456), pp.815–36.

Friston, K.J. et al., 1997. Psychophysiological and modulatory interactions in neuroimaging. *NeuroImage*, 6(3), pp.218–229.

Gilbert, C.D. & Sigman, M., 2007. Brain states: top-down influences in sensory processing. *Neuron*, 54(5), pp.677–96.

Glimcher, P.W., 2011. *Foundations of Neuroeconomic Analysis*, Oxford University Press.

Glimcher, P.W., Dorris, M.C. & Bayer, H.M., 2005. Physiological utility theory and the neuroeconomics of choice. *Games and economic behavior*, 52(2), pp.213–256.

Grill-spector, K., Henson, R. & Martin, A., 2006. Repetition and the brain: neural models of stimulus-speci c effects. *Trends in Cognitive Sciences*, 10(1), pp.17–19.

Güth, W., Schmittberger, R. & Schwarze, B., 1982. An experimental analysis of ultimatum bargaining. *Journal of Economic Behavior & Organization*, 3(4), pp.367–388.

Harel, N., 2012. Ultra high resolution fMRI at ultra-high field. *NeuroImage*, 62(2), pp.1024–1028.

Haxby, J. V et al., 2001. Distributed and overlapping representations of faces and objects in ventral temporal cortex. *Science (New York, N.Y.)*, 293(5539), pp.2425–2430.

Haxby, J. V., 2012. Multivariate pattern analysis of fMRI: The early beginnings. *NeuroImage*, 62(2), pp.852–855.

von Helmholtz, H., 1867. *Handbuch der physiologischen Optik*, Voss.

Henrich, J. et al., 2001. In search of Homo economicus: Behavioral experiments in 15 small-scale societies. *American Economic Review*, 91(2), pp.73–84.

Holland, P.C. & Gallagher, M., 2004. Amygdala-frontal interactions and reward expectancy. *Current opinion in neurobiology*, 14(2), pp.148–55.

Horvitz, J.C., 2000. Mesolimbocortical and nigrostriatal dopamine responses to salient non-reward events. *Neuroscience*, 96(4), pp.651–6.

Hsu, M. et al., 2005. Neural systems responding to degrees of uncertainty in human decision-making. - Supporting material. *Science (New York, N.Y.)*, 310(5754), pp.1680–3.

Huettel, S. a et al., 2006. Neural signatures of economic preferences for risk and ambiguity. *Neuron*, 49(5), pp.765–75.

Izuma, K., Saito, D.N. & Sadato, N., 2008. Processing of social and monetary rewards in the human striatum. *Neuron*, 58(2), pp.284–294.

Johnson, N.D. & Mislin, A.A., 2011. Trust games: A meta-analysis. *Journal of Economic Psychology*, 32(5), pp.865–889.

Kable, J.W. & Glimcher, P.W., 2009. The Neurobiology of Decision: Consensus and Controversy. *Neuron*, 63(6), pp.733–745.

Kahneman, D. & Tversky, A., 1984. Choices, values, and frames. *American psychologist*, 39(4), pp.341–350.

Kahneman, D. & Tversky, A., 1979. Prospect Theory: An Analysis of Decision under Risk. *Econometrica*, 47(2), p.263.

Kampe, K.K. et al., 2001. Reward value of attractiveness and gaze. *Nature*, 413(6856), p.589.

Kim, T. et al., 2012. Modulation of V1 Spike Response by Temporal Interval of Spatiotemporal Stimulus Sequence. *PLoS ONE*, 7(10).

King-Casas, B. et al., 2005. Getting to know you: reputation and trust in a two-person economic exchange. *Science (New York, N.Y.)*, 308(5718), pp.78–83.

Klein, J.T. & Platt, M.L., 2013. Social information signaling by neurons in primate striatum. *Current Biology*, 23(8), pp.691–696.

Knight, F., 1921. Risk, Uncertainty, and Profit. *Hart Schaffner Marx prize essays*, XXXI, pp.1–173.

Knoch, D., Pascual-Leone, A., et al., 2006. Diminishing reciprocal fairness by disrupting the right prefrontal cortex. *Science (New York, N.Y.)*, 314(5800), pp.829–32.

Knoch, D., Gianotti, L.R.R., et al., 2006. Disruption of right prefrontal cortex by low-frequency repetitive transcranial magnetic stimulation induces risk-taking behavior. *The Journal of neuroscience : the official journal of the Society for Neuroscience*, 26(24), pp.6469–72.

Knoch, D. et al., 2008. Studying the neurobiology of social interaction with transcranial direct current stimulation--the example of punishing unfairness. *Cerebral cortex (New York, N.Y. : 1991)*, 18(9), pp.1987–90.

Knutson, B., Adams, C.M., et al., 2001. Anticipation of increasing monetary reward selectively recruits nucleus accumbens. *The Journal of neuroscience : the official journal of the Society for Neuroscience*, 21(16), p.RC159.

Knutson, B., Fong, G.W., et al., 2001. Dissociation of reward anticipation and outcome with event-related fMRI. *Neuroreport*, 12(17), pp.3683–7.

Kok, P. et al., 2012. Attention reverses the effect of prediction in silencing sensory signals. *Cerebral Cortex*, 22(9), pp.2197–2206.

Kolling, N., Wittmann, M. & Rushworth, M.F.S., 2014. Multiple Neural Mechanisms of Decision Making and Their Competition under Changing Risk Pressure. *Neuron*, 81(5), pp.1190–202.

Krajbich, I., Armel, C. & Rangel, A., 2010. Visual fixations and the computation and comparison of value in simple choice. *Nature neuroscience*, 13(10), pp.1292–8.

Krajbich, I. & Rangel, A., 2011. Multialternative drift-diffusion model predicts the relationship between visual fixations and choice in value-based decisions. *Proceedings of the National Academy of Sciences of the United States of America*, 108(33), pp.13852–7.

Krueger, F. et al., 2007. Neural correlates of trust. *Proceedings of the National Academy of Sciences of the United States of America*, 104(50), pp.20084–20089.

Lauharatanahirun, N., Christopoulos, G.I. & King-Casas, B., 2012. Neural computations underlying social risk sensitivity. *Frontiers in Human Neuroscience*, 6(August), p.213.

Lauritzen, M., 2005. Reading vascular changes in brain imaging: is dendritic calcium the key? *Nature reviews. Neuroscience*, 6(1), pp.77–85.

LeDoux, J., 2007. The amygdala. *Current biology : CB*, 17(20), pp.R868–74.

Lee, D., 2008. Game theory and neural basis of social decision making. *Nature neuroscience*, 11(4), pp.404–409.

Lee, T.S. & Mumford, D., 2003. Hierarchical Bayesian inference in the visual cortex. *Journal of the Optical Society of America. A, Optics, image science, and vision*, 20(7), pp.1434–1448.

Leiby, M.L., 2009. Wartime Sexual Violence in Guatemala and Peru. *International Studies Quarterly*, 53(2), pp.445–468.

Levy, I. et al., 2010. Neural representation of subjective value under risk and ambiguity. *Journal of neurophysiology*, 103(2), pp.1036–47.

Lieberman, M.D., 2007. Social cognitive neuroscience: a review of core processes. *Annual review of psychology*, 58, pp.259–89.

Logothetis, N.K., 2008. What we can do and what we cannot do with fMRI. *Nature*, 453(7197), pp.869–78.

Markowitz, H., 1952. Portfolio Selection. *The Journal of Finance*, 7(1), pp.77–91.

Markowitz, H., 1959. *Portfolio selection: efficient diversification of investments*, New Haven, CT: Cowles Foundation.

Matsumoto, M. & Hikosaka, O., 2007. Lateral habenula as a source of negative reward signals in dopamine neurons. *Nature*, 447(7148), pp.1111–5.

Matsumoto, M. & Hikosaka, O., 2009. Two types of dopamine neuron distinctly convey positive and negative motivational signals. *Nature*, 459(7248), pp.837–41.

Matsumura, M. et al., 1992. Visual and oculomotor functions of monkey subthalamic nucleus. *J Neurophysiol*, 67(6), pp.1615–1632.

McCabe, K. et al., 2001. A functional imaging study of cooperation in two-person reciprocal exchange. *Proceedings of the National Academy of Sciences of the United States of America*, 98(20), pp.11832–11835.

McClure, S.M., Berns, G.S. & Montague, P.R., 2003. Temporal prediction errors in a passive learning task activate human striatum. *Neuron*, 38(2), pp.339–46.

McGaugh, J.L., 2004. The amygdala modulates the consolidation of memories of emotionally arousing experiences. *Annual review of neuroscience*, 27, pp.1–28.

McKay, L.S. et al., 2012. Do distinct atypical cortical networks process biological motion information in adults with Autism Spectrum Disorders? *NeuroImage*, 59(2), pp.1524–33.

McLaren, D.G. et al., 2012. A generalized form of context-dependent psychophysiological interactions (gPPI): a comparison to standard approaches. *NeuroImage*, 61(4), pp.1277–86.

Mende-Siedlecki, P., Said, C.P. & Todorov, A., 2012. The social evaluation of faces: a meta-analysis of functional neuroimaging studies. *Social cognitive and affective neuroscience*, 80.

Menon, V. & Uddin, L.Q., 2010. Saliency, switching, attention and control: a network model of insula function. *Brain structure & function*, 214(5-6), pp.655–67.

Metereau, E. & Dreher, J.-C., 2013. Cerebral correlates of salient prediction error for different rewards and punishments. *Cerebral cortex (New York, N.Y. : 1991)*, 23(2), pp.477–87.

Meyer, T. & Olson, C.R., 2011. Statistical learning of visual transitions in monkey inferotemporal cortex. *Proceedings of the National Academy of Sciences*, 108(48), pp.19401–19406.

Miller, E.K. & Cohen, J.D., 2001. An integrative theory of prefrontal cortex function. *Annual review of neuroscience*, 24, pp.167–202.

Mirenowicz, J. & Schultz, W., 1994. Importance of unpredictability for reward responses in primate dopamine neurons. *J Neurophysiol*, 72(2), pp.1024–1027.

Montague, P.R., Dayan, P. & Sejnowski, T.J., 1996. A framework for mesencephalic dopamine systems based on predictive Hebbian learning. *The Journal of neuroscience : the official journal of the Society for Neuroscience*, 16(5), pp.1936–47.

Muckli, L. et al., 2005. Primary visual cortex activity along the apparent-motion trace reflects illusory perception. *PLoS biology*, 3(8), p.e265.

Muckli, L., 2010. What are we missing here? Brain imaging evidence for higher cognitive functions in primary visual cortex V1. *International Journal of Imaging Systems and Technology*, 20(2), pp.131–139.

Muckli, L. & Petro, L.S., 2013. Network interactions: non-geniculate input to V1. *Current opinion in neurobiology*, 23(2), pp.195–201.

Nash, J.F., 1950. Equilibrium Points in N-Person Games. *Proceedings of the National Academy of Sciences of the United States of America*, 36(1), pp.48–9.

Von Neumann, J. & Morgenstern, O., 1944. *Theory of Games and Economic Behavior*,

Nicolle, A. et al., 2012. An Agent Independent Axis for Executed and Modeled Choice in Medial Prefrontal Cortex. *Neuron*, 75(6), pp.1114–1121.

Niki, H. & Watanabe, M., 1976. Cingulate unit activity and delayed response. *Brain research*, 110(2), pp.381–6.

Nishijo, H., Ono, T. & Nishino, H., 1988. Single neuron responses in amygdala of alert monkey during complex sensory stimulation with affective significance. *J. Neurosci.*, 8(10), pp.3570–3583.

Niv, Y., Duff, M.O. & Dayan, P., 2005. Dopamine, uncertainty and TD learning. *Behavioral and brain functions : BBF*, 1(1), p.6.

Niv, Y. & Schoenbaum, G., 2008. Dialogues on prediction errors. *Trends in cognitive sciences*, 12(7), pp.265–72.

Noudoost, B. & Moore, T., 2011. Control of visual cortical signals by prefrontal dopamine. *Nature*, 474(7351), pp.372–5.

O'Neill, M. & Schultz, W., 2010. Coding of Reward Risk by Orbitofrontal Neurons Is Mostly Distinct from Coding of Reward Value. *Neuron*, 68(4), pp.789–800.

O'Neill, M. & Schultz, W., 2013. Risk prediction error coding in orbitofrontal neurons. *The Journal of neuroscience : the official journal of the Society for Neuroscience*, 33(40), pp.15810–4.

O'Reilly, J.X. et al., 2012. Tools of the trade: psychophysiological interactions and functional connectivity. *Social cognitive and affective neuroscience*, 7(5), pp.604–9.

Olivola, C.Y. & Todorov, A., 2010. Elected in 100 milliseconds: Appearance-based trait inferences and voting. *Journal of Nonverbal Behavior*, 34(2), pp.83–110.

den Ouden, H.E.M. et al., 2009. A dual role for prediction error in associative learning. *Cerebral cortex (New York, N.Y. : 1991)*, 19(5), pp.1175–1185.

den Ouden, H.E.M. et al., 2010. Striatal Prediction Error Modulates Cortical Coupling. *Journal of Neuroscience*, 30(9), pp.3210–3219.

den Ouden, H.E.M., Kok, P. & de Lange, F.P., 2012. How prediction errors shape perception, attention, and motivation. *Frontiers in psychology*, 3(December), p.548.

Padoa-Schioppa, C. & Assad, J. a, 2006. Neurons in the orbitofrontal cortex encode economic value. *Nature*, 441(7090), pp.223–6.

Pan, W.-X. et al., 2005. Dopamine cells respond to predicted events during classical conditioning: evidence for eligibility traces in the reward-learning network. *The Journal of neuroscience : the official journal of the Society for Neuroscience*, 25(26), pp.6235–42.

Paulus, M.P. & Stein, M.B., 2006. An Insular View of Anxiety. *Biological Psychiatry*, 60(4), pp.383–387.

Peelen, M. V & Downing, P.E., 2007. The neural basis of visual body perception. *Nature reviews. Neuroscience*, 8(8), pp.636–48.

Peelen, M. V & Kastner, S., 2011. A neural basis for real-world visual search in human occipitotemporal cortex. *Proceedings of the National Academy of Sciences of the United States of America*, 108(29), pp.12125–12130.

Perrett, D.I. et al., 2009. Seeing the future: Natural image sequences produce "anticipatory" neuronal activity and bias perceptual report. *Quarterly journal of experimental psychology (2006)*, 62(11), pp.2081–2104.

Pessiglione, M. et al., 2006. Dopamine-dependent prediction errors underpin reward-seeking behaviour in humans. *Nature*, 442(7106), pp.1042–5.

Pessoa, L. & Adolphs, R., 2010. Emotion processing and the amygdala: from a "low road" to "many roads" of evaluating biological significance. *Nature reviews. Neuroscience*, 11(11), pp.773–83.

Petro, L.S., Vizioli, L. & Muckli, L., 2014. Contributions of cortical feedback to sensory processing in primary visual cortex. *Frontiers in Psychology*, 5.

Phan, K.L. et al., 2010. Reputation for reciprocity engages the brain reward center. *Proceedings of the National Academy of Sciences of the United States of America*, 107(29), pp.13099–13104.

Philiastides, M.G., 2010. A mechanistic account of value computation in the human brain. *Proceedings of the ....*

Philiastides, M.G. et al., 2011. Causal role of dorsolateral prefrontal cortex in human perceptual decision making. *Current biology : CB*, 21(11), pp.980–3.

Philiastides, M.G. & Sajda, P., 2006. Temporal characterization of the neural correlates of perceptual decision making in the human brain. *Cerebral Cortex (New York, N.Y.: 1991)*, 16(4), pp.509–518.

Preuschoff, K. & Bossaerts, P., 2007. Adding prediction risk to the theory of reward learning. *Annals of the New York Academy of Sciences*, 1104, pp.135–46.

Preuschoff, K., Bossaerts, P. & Quartz, S.R., 2006. Neural differentiation of expected reward and risk in human subcortical structures. *Neuron*, 51(3), pp.381–90.

Preuschoff, K., Quartz, S.R. & Bossaerts, P., 2008. Human insula activation reflects risk prediction errors as well as risk. *The Journal of neuroscience : the official journal of the Society for Neuroscience*, 28(11), pp.2745–2752.

Rademacher, L. et al., 2010. Dissociation of neural networks for anticipation and consumption of monetary and social rewards. *NeuroImage*, 49(4), pp.3276–3285.

Rangel, A., Camerer, C. & Montague, P.R., 2008. A framework for studying the neurobiology of value-based decision making. *Nature Reviews Neuroscience*, 9(7), pp.545–556.

Rao, R.P. & Ballard, D.H., 1999. Predictive coding in the visual cortex: a functional interpretation of some extra-classical receptive-field effects. *Nature neuroscience*, 2(1), pp.79–87.

Ratcliff, R., 1978. A theory of memory retrieval. *Psychological Review*, 85(2), pp.59–108.

Ratcliff, R. & McKoon, G., 2008. The diffusion decision model: theory and data for two-choice decision tasks. *Neural computation*, 20(4), pp.873–922.

Redgrave, P., Prescott, T.J. & Gurney, K., 1999. Is the short-latency dopamine response too short to signal reward error? *Trends in neurosciences*, 22(4), pp.146–51.

Rescorla, R.A. & Wagner, A.R., 1972. A theory of Pavlovian conditioning: Variations in the effectiveness of reinforcement and nonreinforcement. *Classical Conditioning II: Current Research and Theory*, pp.64–99.

Rezlescu, C. et al., 2012. Unfakeable facial configurations affect strategic choices in trust games with or without information about past behavior. *PLoS ONE*, 7(3).

Rilling, J. et al., 2002. A neural basis for social cooperation. *Neuron*, 35(2), pp.395–405.

Rilling, J.K. et al., 2004. The neural correlates of theory of mind within interpersonal interactions. *NeuroImage*, 22(4), pp.1694–703.

Roebroeck, A., Formisano, E. & Goebel, R., 2005. Mapping directed influence over the brain using Granger causality and fMRI. *NeuroImage*, 25(1), pp.230–42.

Romo, R. & Schultz, W., 1990. Dopamine neurons of the monkey midbrain: contingencies of responses to active touch during self-initiated arm movements. *Journal of neurophysiology*, 63(3), pp.592–606.

Rudorf, S., Preuschoff, K. & Weber, B., 2012. Neural Correlates of Anticipation Risk Reflect Risk Preferences. *Journal of Neuroscience*, 32(47), pp.16683–16692.

Ruff, C.C. & Fehr, E., 2014. The neurobiology of rewards and values in social decision making. *Nature reviews. Neuroscience*, 15(July), pp.549–562.

Rutledge, R.B. et al., 2010. Testing the reward prediction error hypothesis with an axiomatic model. *The Journal of neuroscience : the official journal of the Society for Neuroscience*, 30(40), pp.13525–13536.

Said, C.P., Baron, S.G. & Todorov, A., 2009. Nonlinear amygdala response to face trustworthiness: contributions of high and low spatial frequency information. *Journal of cognitive neuroscience*, 21(3), pp.519–28.

Sally, D., 1995. Conversation and Cooperation in Social Dilemmas: A Meta-Analysis of Experiments from 1958 to 1992. *Rationality and Society*, 7(1), pp.58–92.

Sanfey, A.G., 2007. Social decision-making: insights from game theory and neuroscience. *Science (New York, N.Y.)*, 318(5850), pp.598–602.

Sanfey, A.G. et al., 2003. The neural basis of economic decision-making in the Ultimatum Game. *Science (New York, N.Y.)*, 300(5626), pp.1755–8.

Sato, M. & Hikosaka, O., 2002. Role of primate substantia nigra pars reticulata in reward-oriented saccadic eye movement. *The Journal of neuroscience : the official journal of the Society for Neuroscience*, 22(6), pp.2363–73.

Schippers, M.B., Renken, R. & Keysers, C., 2011. The effect of intra- and inter-subject variability of hemodynamic responses on group level Granger causality analyses. *NeuroImage*, 57(1), pp.22–36.

Schlicht, E.J. et al., 2010. Human wagering behavior depends on opponents' faces. *PLoS ONE*, 5(7).

Schultz, W. et al., 2008. Explicit neural signals reflecting reward uncertainty. *Philosophical transactions of the Royal Society of London. Series B, Biological sciences*, 363(1511), pp.3801–11.

Schultz, W., 2013. Updating dopamine reward signals. *Current opinion in neurobiology*, 23(2), pp.229–38.

Schultz, W., Dayan, P. & Montague, P.R., 1997. A neural substrate of prediction and reward. *Science (New York, N.Y.)*, 275(June 1994), pp.1593–1599.

Seeley, W.W. et al., 2007. Dissociable intrinsic connectivity networks for salience processing and executive control. *The Journal of neuroscience : the official journal of the Society for Neuroscience*, 27(9), pp.2349–2356.

Serences, J.T., 2008. Value-based modulations in human visual cortex. *Neuron*, 60(6), pp.1169–81.

Serences, J.T. & Saproo, S., 2010. Population response profiles in early visual cortex are biased in favor of more valuable stimuli. *Journal of neurophysiology*, 104(1), pp.76–87.

Sereno, M.I. et al., 1995. Borders of multiple visual areas in humans revealed by functional magnetic resonance imaging. *Science (New York, N.Y.)*, 268(5212), pp.889–93.

Sergerie, K., Chochol, C. & Armony, J.L., 2008. The role of the amygdala in emotional processing: a quantitative meta-analysis of functional neuroimaging studies. *Neuroscience and biobehavioral reviews*, 32(4), pp.811–30.

Sescousse, G., Redouté, J. & Dreher, J.-C., 2010. The Architecture of Reward Value Coding in the Human Orbitofrontal Cortex. *The Journal of Neuroscience*, 30(39), pp.13095–13104.

Seth, A.K., 2013. Interoceptive inference, emotion, and the embodied self. *Trends in cognitive sciences*, 17(11), pp.565–73.

Seth, A.K., Barrett, A.B. & Barnett, L., 2015. Granger Causality Analysis in Neuroscience and Neuroimaging. *Journal of Neuroscience*, 35(8), pp.3293–3297.

Seymour, B. et al., 2007. Differential encoding of losses and gains in the human striatum. *The Journal of neuroscience : the official journal of the Society for Neuroscience*, 27(18), pp.4826–31.

Seymour, B. et al., 2004. Temporal difference models describe higher-order learning in humans. *Nature*, 429(6992), pp.664–7.

Shuler, M.G. & Bear, M.F., 2006. Reward timing in the primary visual cortex. *Science (New York, N.Y.)*, 311(5767), pp.1606–9.

Singer, T. et al., 2004. Brain responses to the acquired moral status of faces. *Neuron*, 41(4), pp.653–62.

Singer, T., Critchley, H.D. & Preuschoff, K., 2009. A common role of insula in feelings, empathy and uncertainty. *Trends in cognitive sciences*, 13(8), pp.334–40.

Sirotin, Y.B. & Das, A., 2009. Anticipatory haemodynamic signals in sensory cortex not predicted by local neuronal activity. *Nature*, 457(7228), pp.475–9.

Smith, F.W. & Muckli, L., 2010. Nonstimulated early visual areas carry information about surrounding context. *Proceedings of the National Academy of Sciences of the United States of America*, 107(46), pp.20099–20103.

Smith, M.L., Gosselin, F. & Schyns, P.G., 2012. Measuring Internal Representations from Behavioral and Brain Data. *Current Biology*, 22(3), pp.191–196.

Späti, J. et al., 2014. Functional lateralization of the anterior insula during feedback processing. *Human brain mapping*, 35(9), pp.4428–39.

Spratling, M.W., 2008. Reconciling predictive coding and biased competition models of cortical function. *Frontiers in computational neuroscience*, 2, p.4.

Spreckelmeyer, K.N. et al., 2009. Anticipation of monetary and social reward differently activates mesolimbic brain structures in men and women. *Social Cognitive and Affective Neuroscience*, 4(2), pp.158–165.

Stalnaker, T. a, Cooch, N.K. & Schoenbaum, G., 2015. What the orbitofrontal cortex does not do. *Nature Neuroscience*, 18(5), pp.620–627.

Stănişor, L. et al., 2013. A unified selection signal for attention and reward in primary visual cortex. *Proceedings of the National Academy of Sciences of the United States of America*, 110(22), pp.9136–41.

Striepens, N. et al., 2014. Oxytocin enhances attractiveness of unfamiliar female faces independent of the dopamine reward system. *Psychoneuroendocrinology*, 39(1), pp.74–87.

Sugrue, L.P., Corrado, G.S. & Newsome, W.T., 2005. Choosing the greater of two goods: neural currencies for valuation and decision making. *Nature reviews. Neuroscience*, 6(5), pp.363–75.

Sutton, R.S. & Barto, A.G., 1998. *Introduction to Reinforcement Learning*, MIT Press.

Swanson, L.W. & Petrovich, G.D., 1998. What is the amygdala? *Trends in neurosciences*, 21(8), pp.323–331.

Tabibnia, G., Satpute, A.B. & Lieberman, M.D., 2008. The Sunny Side of Fairness. *Psychological Science*, 19(4), pp.339–347.

Takahashi, Y.K. et al., 2011. Expectancy-related changes in firing of dopamine neurons depend on orbitofrontal cortex. *Nature Neuroscience*, 14(12), pp.1590–1597.

Takahashi, Y.K. et al., 2009. The orbitofrontal cortex and ventral tegmental area are necessary for learning from unexpected outcomes. *Neuron*, 62(2), pp.269–80.

Tan, C.O., 2009. Anticipatory changes in regional cerebral hemodynamics: a new role for dopamine? *Journal of neurophysiology*, 101(6), pp.2738–40.

Tingley, D., 2014. Face-Off: Facial Features and Strategic Choice. *Political Psychology*, 35(1), pp.35–55.

Tobler, P.N. et al., 2007. Reward value coding distinct from risk attitude-related uncertainty coding in human reward systems. *Journal of neurophysiology*, 97(2), pp.1621–32.

Tobler, P.N., Fiorillo, C.D. & Schultz, W., 2005. Adaptive coding of reward value by dopamine neurons. *Science (New York, N.Y.)*, 307(5715), pp.1642–5.

Todorov, A., Mende-Siedlecki, P. & Dotsch, R., 2013. Social judgments from faces. *Current opinion in neurobiology*, 23(3), pp.373–80.

Todorov, A. & Oosterhof, N., 2011. Modeling Social Perception of Faces [Social Sciences]. *IEEE Signal Processing Magazine*, 28(2), pp.117–122.

Todorovic, A. et al., 2011. Prior expectation mediates neural adaptation to repeated sounds in the auditory cortex: an MEG study. *The Journal of neuroscience : the official journal of the Society for Neuroscience*, 31(25), pp.9118–9123.

Tremblay, L. & Schultz, W., 1999. Relative reward preference in primate orbitofrontal cortex. *Nature*, 398(6729), pp.704–8.

Voon, V. et al., 2010. Mechanisms underlying dopamine-mediated reward bias in compulsive behaviors. *Neuron*, 65(1), pp.135–142.

Vuilleumier, P., 2005. How brains beware: Neural mechanisms of emotional attention. *Trends in Cognitive Sciences*, 9(12), pp.585–594.

Wandell, B. a & Winawer, J., 2011. Imaging retinotopic maps in the human brain. *Vision research*, 51(7), pp.718–37.

Whalen, P. & Phelps, E.A., 2009. *The human amygdala*, New York: Guilford Press.

Whalen, P.J., 1998. Fear, Vigilance, and Ambiguity: Initial Neuroimaging Studies of the Human Amygdala. *Current Directions in Psychological Science*, 7(6), pp.177–188.

Willis, J. & Todorov, A., 2006. First impressions: making up your mind after a 100-ms exposure to a face. *Psychological science*, 17(7), pp.592–8.

Winston, J.S. et al., 2002. Automatic and intentional brain responses during evaluation of trustworthiness of faces. *Nature neuroscience*, 5(3), pp.277–283.

Wise, R.A. & Rompre, P.P., 1989. Brain dopamine and reward. *Annual review of psychology*, 40, pp.191–225.

Yacubian, J. et al., 2007. Gene-gene interaction associated with neural reward sensitivity. *Proceedings of the National Academy of Sciences of the United States of America*, 104(19), pp.8125–8130.

Zink, C.F. et al., 2003. Human striatal response to salient nonrewarding stimuli. *The Journal*

CPSIA information can be obtained
at www.ICGtesting.com
Printed in the USA
LVHW080547280223
740519LV00015B/204